TEST

D0851180

FOR 250

YOUNG

ADULT

NOVELS

Roberta Gail Shipley

Neal-Schuman Publishers, Inc.
New York   London

Published by Neal-Schuman Publishers, Inc.
100 Varick Street
New York, NY 10013

Printed and bound in the United States of America.

Library of Congress Cataloging-in-Publication Data

Shipley , Roberta Gail .
    Test for 250 young adult novels / by Roberta Gail Shipley .
        p.   cm.
    Includes bibliographical references (p .) and index.
    ISBN 1-55570 - 192 - 2:
    1. Young adult fiction , American--Examinations , questions , etc .
2 . Young adults--Books and reading--Examinations , questions , etc .
I . Title .   II . Title : Test for two hundred fifty young adult novels .
PS374 . Y57S45 1995
813 . 009 ' 9283 -- dc20   94 - 36771
                                                           CIP

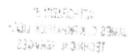

TABLE OF CONTENTS

TABLE OF CONTENTS

ACKNOWLEDGEMENTS

I would like to thank Judy Ingraham whose idea it was to write these tests on young adult novels and who encouraged me to run with her idea.

I would also like to thank Sherry Haun who loaned me all the books I needed out of her school library and for being gracious and understanding about how long I kept them.

INTRODUCTION

The ever-increasing popularity of the "whole language" movement has demonstrated that one of the best ways to help children develop a lifelong love of reading is to connect them with the books that deal with subjects and issues that they are most interested in. Educators and librarians often hope to accomplish this by suggesting good books and encouraging students to read outside the classroom. Some teachers try to stimulate interest in books by making outside reading a way for students to earn extra credit—or even incorporate it into their curriculum by setting up classroom-based, outside reading programs.

But what are the best books for students to choose from? And if involvement in such a program will be a component of a student's grade, how can a teacher make sure that the reading has actually been completed? TESTS FOR 250 YOUNG ADULT NOVELS was developed at Forest Oak Middle School, where I was able to establish this kind of successful reading program with the help of other educators, students, and librarians. The brief, multiple choice tests that replace book reports were specifically designed to be a simple, effective way to motivate students to read and to ascertain whether or not the assignment they selected has been completed. As was the case in my school, this book can help teachers transform uninterested students who simply read dust jackets and wrote book reports based on blurbs previously into committed readers averaging 18 novels a year in class.

The 250 novels for which these tests are designed were selected based on the following criteria: quality of writing, popularity, currency, genre, and multiculturalism. Reading levels range from fourth to ninth grade, and lengths from 70 to 225 pages. The books cover a wide range of reading abilities, everything from titles of interest for reluctant readers, through those that are sure to challenge even the most gifted students. Most of these books have been published within the past few years. Many are award winners, including numerous Newbery and Newbery Honor Award winners, state children's choice selections, ALA Best Books, and ALA Best Books for Reluctant Readers. There are also a number of titles with more mass market appeal. All have been judged to be well-written, with interesting plots and contemporary characters a range of students can relate to. Everything from romance, sports, mystery, thrillers, westerns, and adventure, to friendship, historical fiction and novels dealing with social issues is included.

TESTS FOR 250 YOUNG ADULT NOVELS is arranged alphabetically by title, with indexes listing author and title, and titles by subject. There are no "trick" questions. Rather, questions follow the sequence of the plot so that teachers can measure how far along the student has read. In order to make the tests user-friendly, there are only two answer keys. You might want to set up the program and testing procedure by using the following steps:

1. Most of these books are available in inexpensive paperback editions that can be kept in the classroom for use by one teacher and her class, but if at all possible, you might want to base your program in the library. In preparation for special library visits from several different classes, the librarian can lay all of the appropriate books out on a special shelf. Teachers and librarians can work together to purchase books for the program, make book recommendations for students, handle supervision, and provide more encouragement than an educator handling a class alone would be able to. Also, with repeated visits, students

might grow to feel more comfortable in the library setting and eventually come to think of it as a place to return to find good books—even when there is no test to take!

2. Designate one class period every two weeks as ⅓oLibrary Day¼o whether or not you plan to incorporate this program with the library. Have students select a book and read the back cover and the first page of the book before checking it out to make sure it is not too difficult for them to read.

3. After students have chosen their desired title, let them use the rest of the class period to read and get a good start on their book. Have them finish the books on their own.

4. Have students find out how many pages they must read a day to finish their books within two weeks. If they read daily divide the number of pages by 14. If they do not want to read on weekends have them divide the number of pages by 10.

5. If you don't want to make photocopies, why not put each test in a plastic paper saver. You can get these paper savers at office supply stores. When the test is inside the plastic, the students will know that they should write on their own paper and not on the test. It also keeps the tests clean. Before using the plastic paper savers if a child accidentally wrote on a test no one else could take that test until another copy was made from my original because I only keep one copy of each test on hand. Since I started using these covers I very rarely have had to make copies. File all tests alphabetically by title into a box.

6. At the end of two weeks have the students look up their test in the file box by the title.

7. On their own paper have the students include the title of their book, and the form (A or B). Students should be able to take the test in 5 minutes writing only the letter of the correct answer.

8. On the day the students take the test have them select a new book.

9. Collect the tests from the students. Do not let them grade the tests because there are only two answer keys—I made one form for each title. There isn't a form A and B for each test. Half of the novels have form A for their answer key and the other half of the novels have form B. Two answer keys were made because I thought the students might catch on if all the tests had the same answers. Because there are only two keys the students are not allowed to grade the papers or get their paper back. Every student is told what grade they made, how many they missed, and if they want to see their test and answers again they may but they cannot keep them. If a student does poorly, I discuss the possible reasons for this with them.

Every test contains 10 questions, and I have found that it works best to make each question worth 10 points, for a total of 110. I offer the extra 10 points in case one particular question is confusing to the student. I also do not penalize students for picking shorter books because readers who struggle sometimes work harder than those who can read longer books. It has also been my experience that students at a higher reading level usually choose the more difficult books on their own.

250 TESTS FOR YOUNG ADULT READERS is designed as an effective, easy-to-use, and accurate way to measure a student's reading progress. My hope is that these tests are a tool which may lead teachers to feel more comfortable making the reading program a higher percentage of a student's grade, sending the right message about the importance of outside reading. The simplicity of this test system can also free up valuable time that teachers can use to better prepare for the lessons they will give during class time. Happy testing!

BIBLIOGRAPHY

Aaron, Chester. *Alex, Who Won His War.* Walker and Co., 1991, 156 pages.

Adler, C.S. *In Our House Scott Is My Brother.* Macmillan, 1980, 139 pages.

Aiken, Joan. *Night Fall.* Holt, Rinehart and Winston, 1969, 116 pages.

Aiken, Joan. *The Wolves of Willoughby Chase.* Doubleday, 1962, 168 pages.

Alcock, Vivien. *A Kind of Thief.* Delacorte Press, 1991, 179 pages.

Alcock, Vivien. *The Monster Garden.* Delacorte Press, 1988, 160 pages.

Angell, Judi. *Don't Rent My Room.* Bantam, 1990, 138 pages.

Angell, Judi. *Leave the Cooking to Me.* Bantam, 1990, 185 pages.

Avi. *Devil's Race.* Avon, 1984, 160 pages.

Avi. *The Fighting Ground.* J.B. Lippincott, 1984, 157 pages.

Avi. *Nothing But the Truth.* Orchard Books, 1991, 177 pages.

Avi. *Something Upstairs.* Orchard Books, 1988, 120 pages.

Avi. *S.O.R. Losers.* Bradbury Press, 1984, 90 pages.

Avi. *The True Confessions of Charlotte Doyle.* Orchard Books, 1990, 215 pages.

Avi. *Windcatcher.* Bradbury Press, 1991, 124 pages.

Banks, Lynne Reid. *The Indian in the Cupboard.* Doubleday, 1980, 181 pages.

Beatty, Patricia. *The Coach That Never Came.* William Morrow, 1985, 164 pages.

Beatty, Patricia. *Turn Homeward Hannalee.* William Morrow, 1984, 193 pages.

Bechard, Margaret. *My Sister, My Science Report.* Viking, 1990, 102 pages.

Bennett, Jay. *Coverup.* Watts, 1991, 144 pages.

Bennett, Jay. *The Skeleton Man.* Watts, 1986, 170 pages.

Betancourt, Jeanne. *More Than Meets the Eye.* Bantam, 1990, 166 pages.

Bloom, Judy. *Deenie.* Bradbury Press, 1973, 159 pages.

Blos, Joan W. *Brothers of the Heart.* Charles Scribner's Sons, 1985, 162 pages.

Bradshaw, Gillian. *The Dragon and the Thief.* Greenwillow, 1991, 154 pages.

Brancato, Robin F. *Sweet Bells Jangled Out of Tune.* Knopf, 982, 200 pages.

Brittain, Bill. *Dr. Dredd's Wagon of Wonders.* Harper and Row, 1987, 179 pages.

Brittain, Bill. *The Fantastic Freshman.* Harper and Row, 1988, 151 pages.

Brittain, Bill. *My Buddy, the King.* Harper and Row, 1989, 135 pages.

Brittain, Bill. *Professor Popkin's Prodigious Polish.* Harper and Row, 1990, 152 pages.

Brittain, Bill. *Who Knew There'd Be Ghosts?* Harper and Row, 1985, 119 pages.

Brittain, Bill. *The Wish Giver.* Harper and Row, 1983, 181 pages.

Brown, Alan. *Lost Boys Never Say Die.* Delacorte Press, 1989.

Buffie, Margaret. *The Haunting of Francis Rain.* Scholastic Inc., 1989, 196 pages.

Bunting, Eve. *Is Anybody There?* J.B. Lippincott, 1988, 170 pages.

Bunting, Eve. *Such Nice Kids.* Clarion Books, 1990, 120 pages.

Byars, Betsy. *Bingo Brown, Gypsy Lover.* Viking, 1990, 122 pages.

Byars, Betsy. *A Blossom Promise.* Delacorte Press, 1987, 145 pages.

Campbell, Eric. *The Place of Lions.* Harcourt Brace Jovanovich, 1991, 185 pages.

Cannon, A.E. *Shadow Brothers.* Delacorte Press, 1990, 179 pages.

Carter, Alden R. *Robo Dad.* G.P. Putnam's Sons, 1990, 144 pages.

Caseley, Judith. *Kisses.* Knopf, 1990, 186 pages.

Chetwin, Grace. *Child of the Air.* Bradbury Press, 1991, 231 pages.

Chetwin, Grace. *Collidescope.* Bradbury Press, 1990, 221 pages.

Cleary, Beverly. *Strider.* Morrow, 1991, 179 pages.

Conford, Ellen. *Dear Mom, Get Me Out of Here.* Little, Brown and Co., 1992, 160 pages.

Conford, Ellen. *A Royal Pain.* Scholastic Inc., 1986, 171 pages.

Conrad, Pam. *My Daniel.* Harper and Row, 1989, 137 pages.

Conrad, Pam. *Prairie Songs.* Harper and Row, 1985, 167 pages.

Conrad, Pam. *Stone Words.* Harper and Row, 1990, 130 pages.

Cooney, Caroline B. *The Face On the Milk Carton.* Bantam, 1990, 184 pages.

Cooney, Caroline B. *Family Reunion.* Bantam, 1989, 169 pages.

Cooney, Caroline B. *Flight #116 Is Down.* Scholastic Inc., 1992, 201 pages.

Cooney, Caroline B. *The Party's Over.* Scholastic Inc., 1991, 187 pages.

Cooper, Susan. *Greenwitch.* Atheneum, 1974, 147 pages.

Cormier, Robert. *The Chocolate War.* G.K. Hall, 1988, 344 pages.

Coville, Bruce. *Jeremy Thatcher, Dragon Hatcher.* Harcourt Brace Jovanovich, 1991, 148 pages.

Coville, Bruce. *My Teacher Glows In the Dark.* Minstrel Books, 1991, 144 pages.

Coville, Bruce. *My Teacher Is An Alien.* Minstrel Books, 1990.

Crew, Linda. *Children of the River.* Delacorte Press, 1989, 213 pages.

Cusick, Richie Tankersley. *The Lifeguard.* Scholastic Inc., 1988, 192 pages.

Cusick, Richie Tankersley. *Trick or Treat.* Scholastic Inc., 1989, 208 pages.

Danziger, Paula. *Can You Sue Your Parents For Malpractice?* Delacorte Press, 1979, 152 pages.

Danziger, Paula. *This Place Has No Atmosphere.* Delacorte Press, 1986, 156 pages.

Davis, Jenny. *Checking On the Moon.* Orchard Books, 1991, 208 pages.

Deaver, Julie Reece. *Say Goodnight, Gracie.* Harper and Row, 1988, 214 pages.

DeClement, Barthe. *Breaking Out.* Delacorte Press, 1991, 130 pages.

DeClement, Barthe. *Five-Finger Discount.* Delacorte Press, 1989, 131 pages.

DeClement, Barthe. *Monkey See, Monkey Do.* Delacorte Press, 1990, 146 pages.

Duder, Tessa. *In Lane Three, Alex Archer.* Houghton Mifflin C., 1987, 175 pages.

Duncan, Lois. *Don't Look Behind You.* Laurel Leaf/Dell Pub., 1989, 179 pages.

Duncan, Lois. *I Know What You Did Last Summer.* Little, Brown, 1973, 199 pages.

Duncan, Lois. *The Third Eye.* Little, Brown, 1984, 220 pages.

Duncan, Lois. *The Twisted Window.* Delacorte Press, 1987, 183 pages.

Dygard, Thomas J. *Forward Pass.* Morrow, 1989, 186 pages.

Dygard, Thomas J. *Tournament Upstart.* Morrow, 1984, 208 pages.

Dygard, Thomas J. *Wilderness Peril.* Morrow, 1985, 194 pages.

Ehrlick, Amy. *Where It Stops, Nobody Knows.* Dial Books, 1988, 212 pages.

Ellis, Anne Leo. *The Dragon of Middlethorpe.* Henry Holt and Co., 1991, 180 pages.

Fenner, Carol. *Randall's Wall.* Margaret K. McElderry Books, 1991, 85 pages.

Fleischman, Paul. *The Borning Room.* Harper Collins, 1991, 101 pages.

Fleischman, Paul. *Saturnalia.* Harper and Row, 1990, 113 pages.

Fleischman, Sid. *Jim Ugly.* Greenwillow, 1992, 130 pages.

Foley, June. *Susanna Siegelbaum Gives Up Guys.* Scholastic Inc., 1991, 152 pages.

Fox, Paula. *One-Eyed Cat.* Bradbury Press, 1984, 216 pages.

Garland, Sherry. *Song of the Buffalo Boy.* Harcourt Brace, 1992, 249 pages.

Geller, Mark. *The Strange Case of the Reluctant Partners.* Harper and Row, 1990, 88 pages.

George, Jean Craighead. *The Cry of the Crow.* Harper and Row, 1980, 149 pages.

George, Jean Craighead. *Shark Beneath the Reef.* Harper and Row, 1989, 182 pages.

Giff, Patricia Reilly. *The Gift of the Pirate Queen.* Delacorte Press, 1982, 164 pages.

Girion, Barbara. *Indian Summer.* Scholastic Inc., 1990, 183 pages.

Greenberg, Jan. *No Dragons to Slay.* Farrar, Straus, Giroux, 1983, 119 pages.

Greer and Ruddick. *Max and Me and the Time Machine.* Harcourt Brace Jovanovich, 1983, 114 pages.

Greer and Ruddick. *Max and Me and the Wild West.* Harcourt Brace Jovanovich, 1988, 138 pages.

Grove, Vicki. *Junglerama.* Putnam, 1989, 192 pages.

Hahn, Mary Downing. *Dead Man in Indian Creek.* Clarion Books, 1990, 130 pages.

Hahn, Mary Downing. *December Stillness.* Clarion Books, 1988, 181 pages.

Hahn, Mary Downing. *The Doll in the Garden.* Clarion Books, 1989, 128 pages.

Hahn, Mary Downing. *The Spanish Kidnapping Disaster.* Clarion Books, 1991, 132 pages.

Hall, Barbara. *Dixie Storms.* Harcourt Brace Jovanovich, 1990, 197 pages.

Hall, Lynn. *Dagmar Schultz and the Green-Eyed Monster.* Macmillan Child Group, 1991, 80 pages.

Hall, Lynn. *Killing Freeze.* Morrow, 1988, 120 pages.

Hall, Lynn. *Murder in a Pig's Eye.* Harcourt Brace Jovanovich, 1990, 116 pages.

Hall, Lynn. *The Tormenters.* Harcourt Brace Jovanovich, 1990, 102 pages.

Hamm, Diane Johnston. *Bunkhouse Journal.* Macmillan Child Group, 1990, 96 pages.

Haven, Susan. *Is It Them Or Is It Me?* Putnam, 1990.

Hayden and Kistler. *Has Anyone Seen Allie?* Cobblehill Books, 1991, 124 pages.

Hayes, Daniel. *The Trouble With Lemons.* David R. Godine, 1991, 183 pages.

Hermes, Patricia. *Kevin Corbett Eats Flies.* Harcourt Brace Jovanovich, 1986, 160 pages.

Hinton, S.E. *Rumble Fish.* Delacorte Press, 1975, 122 pages.

Hinton, S.E. *That Was Then, This Is Now.* Viking, 1971, 159 pages.

Ho, Minfong. *Clay Marble.* Farrar, Straus, Giroux, 1991, 163 pages.

Hobbs, Will. *Down River.* Atheneum, 1991, 204 pages.

Holman, Felice. *Slake's Limbo.* Scribner, 1974, 117 pages.

Hughes, Monica. *Invitation to the Game.* Half Moon Books, 1992, 208 pages.

Kaplow, Robert. *Alessandra In Love.* Lippincott, 1989, 153 pages.

Kehret, Peg. *Cages.* Cobblehill Books/Dutton, 1991, 150 pages.

Kerr, M.E. *Dinky Hocker Shoots Smack.* Dell, 1973, 192 pages.

Kerr, M.E. *Fell.* Harper and Row, 1987, 165 pages.

Kerr, M.E. *Fell Back.* Harper and Row, 1989, 181 pages.

Kerr, M.E. *Fell Down.* Harper Collins, 1991, 191 pages.

Killien, Christi. *Rusty Fertlander, Lady's Man.* Houghton Mifflin, 1988, 133 pages.

Korman, Gordon. *Don't Care High.* Scholastic Inc., 1985, 243 pages.

Korman, Gordon. *Losing Joe's Place.* Scholastic Inc., 1990, 192 pages.

Lawrence, Louise. *Andra.* Harper and Row, 1991, 229 pages.

L'Engle, Madeleine. *The Moon By Night.* Ariel Books, Farrar, Straus, 1963, 218 pages.

Leroe, Ellen. *H.O.W.L. High.* Minstrel Books, 1991, 144 pages.

Littke, Lael. *Prom Dress.* Scholastic Inc., 1989, 176 pages.

Littke, Lael. *Shanny On Her Own.* Harcourt Brace Jovanovich, 1985, 179 pages.

Lowry, Lois. *Your Move, J.P.!* Houghton Mifflin, 1990, 122 pages.

Lypsyte, Robert. *The Brave.* Barricade Books, 1991, 215 pages.

Lypsyte, Robert. *One Fat Summer.* Harper and Row, 1977, 152 pages.

Martin, Ann M. *Just a Summer Romance.* Holiday House, 1987, 163 pages.

Matas, Carol. *Lisa's War.* C. Scribner's Sons, 1987. 111 pages.

Mazer, Harry. *Snow Bound.* Dell, 1975, 144 pages.

McCuaig, Sandra. *Blindfold.* Holiday House, 1990, 167 pages.

Milligan, Bryce. *With the Wind, Kevin Dolan.* Corona Pub., 1992, 194 pages.

Monson, A.M. *The Secret of Sanctuary Island.* Lothrop, Lee and Shepard Books, 1991, 164 pages.

Morey, Walt. *Death Walk.* Huron Heron, 1993, 176 pages.

Mowat, Farley. *Lost in the Barrens.* Little, 1956, 244 pages.

Murrow, Lisa Ketchum. *The Ghost of Lost Island.* Holiday House, 1991, 165 pages.

Myers, Walter Dean. *Crystal.* Viking Kestrel, 1987, 198 pages.

Myers, Walter Dean. *Hoops.* Delacorte Press, 1981, 183 pages.

Myers, Walter Dean. *Mouse Rap.* Harper and Row, 1990, 186 pages.

Myers, Walter Dean. *Scorpions.* Harper and Row, 1988, 216 pages.

Naylor, Phyllis Reynolds. *Alice In Rapture, Sort Of.* Atheneum, 1989, 166 pages.

Naylor, Phyllis Reynolds. *Send No Blessings.* Atheneum, 1990, 231 pages.

Nixon, Joan Lowery. *A Candidate For Murder.* Delacorte Press, 1991, 210 pages.

Nixon, Joan Lowery. *Caught In the Act.* Bantam, 1988, 150 pages.

Nixon, Joan Lowery. *Encore*. Bantam, 1990, 196 pages.

Nixon, Joan Lowery. *A Family Apart*. Bantam, 1987, 162 pages.

Nixon, Joan Lowery. *The Gift*. Macmillan, 1983, 86 pages.

Nixon, Joan Lowery. *High Trail To Danger*. Bantam, 1991, 168 pages.

Nixon, Joan Lowery. *The House On Hackman's Hill*. Scholastic Inc., 1985, 126 pages.

Nixon, Joan Lowery. *In the Face of Danger*. Bantam, 1988, 151 pages.

Nixon, Joan Lowery. *Maggie, Too*. Harcourt Brace Jovanovich, 1985, 101 pages.

Nixon, Joan Lowery. *Mystery of the Haunted Woods*. Criterion Books, 1967, 144 pages.

Nixon, Joan Lowery. *Mystery of Hurricane Castle*. Criterion Books, 1964, 144 pages.

Nixon, Joan Lowery. *Overnight Sensation*. Bantam, 1990, 180 pages.

Nixon, Joan Lowery. *A Place to Belong*. Bantam, 1989, 147 pages.

Nixon, Joan Lowery. *Secret Silent Screams*. Delacorte Press, 1988, 180 pages.

Nixon, Joan Lowery. *The Stalker*. Delacorte Press, 1985, 180 pages.

Nixon, Joan Lowery. *Star Baby*. Bantam, 1989.

O'Dell, Scott. *The Serpent Never Sleeps*. Houghton Mifflin, 1987, 227 pages.

O'Dell, Scott. *Sing Down the Moon*. Houghton Mifflin, 1970, 137 pages.

O'Dell, Scott. *The Spanish Smile*. Houghton Mifflin, 1982, 182 pages.

Orlev, Uri. *The Man From the Other Side*. Houghton Mifflin, 1991, 186 pages.

Paterson, Katherine. *Lyddie*. Dutton, 1991, 182 pages.

Paulsen, Gary. *The Boy Who Owned the School*. Orchard Books, 1990, 85 pages.

Paulsen, Gary. *Canyons*. Delacorte Press, 1990, 184 pages.

Paulsen, Gary. *The Cook Camp*. Orchard Books, 1991, 115 pages.

Paulsen, Gary. *The Crossing*. Orchard Books, 1987, 114 pages.

Paulsen, Gary. *Hatchet*. Bradbury Press, 1987, 195 pages.

Paulsen, Gary. *The Island*. Orchard Books, 1988, 202 pages.

Paulsen, Gary. *The Monument*. Delacorte Press, 1991, 151 pages.

Paulsen, Gary. *The Night the White Deer Died*. Delacorte Press, 1990, 104 pages.

Paulsen, Gary. *Popcorn Days and Buttermilk Nights*. E.P. Dutton, 1983, 100 pages.

Paulsen, Gary. *The River*. Delacorte Press, 1991, 132 pages.

Paulsen, Gary. *Tracker*. Bradbury Press, 1984, 90 pages.

Paulsen, Gary. *The Voyage of the Frog*. Orchard Books, 1989, 141 pages.

Paulsen, Gary. *The Winter Room*. Orchard Books, 1989, 103 pages.

Peck, Richard. *Are You in the House Alone?* Viking, 1976, 156 pages.

Petersen, P.J. *Going For the Big One*. Delacorte Press, 1986, 178 pages.

Pevsner, Stella. *How Could You Do It, Diane?* Clarion Books, 1989, 183 pages.

Pevsner, Stella. *The Night the Whole Class Slept Over*. Clarion Books, 1991, 162 pages.

Pfeffer, Beth. *The Year Without Michael*. Bantam, 1987, 164 pages.

Pinkwater, Jill. *Buffalo Brenda*. Macmillan, 1989, 203 pages.

Powell, Randy. *My Underrated Year*. Farrar, Straus, Giroux, 1988, 181 pages.

Rawls, Wilson. *Summer of the Monkeys*. Doubleday, 1976, 239 pages.

Roberts, Willo Davis. *Scared Stiff*. Atheneum, 1991, 188 pages.

Rodda, Emily. *Finders Keepers*. Greenwillow Books, 1990, 184 pages.

Roth, Arthur. *The Iceberg Hermit*. Four Winds Press, 1974, 201 pages.

Ryan, Mary E. *My Sister Is Driving Me Crazy*. Simon and Schuster, 1991, 223 pages.

Sachar, Louis. *The Boy Who Lost His Face*. Alfred A. Knopf, 1989, 198 pages.

Schenker, Dona. *Throw a Hungry Loop*. Alfred A. Knopf, 1990, 114 pages.

Schwartz, Joel L. *Upchuck Summer's Revenge*. Doubleday, 1990.

Service, Pamela F. *Being of Two Minds*. Atheneum, 1991, 169 pages.

Service, Pamela F. *Under Alien Stars*. Atheneum, 1990, 214 pages.

Sharmat, Marjorie. *Are We There Yet?* Laurel-Leaf Books.

Shreve, Susan. *The Gift of the Girl Who Couldn't Hear*. Tambourine Books, 1991, 79 pages.

Sinykin, Sheri Cooper. *Next Thing to Strangers.* Lothrop, Lee and Shepard Books, 1991, 147 pages.

Sleator, William. *Among the Dolls.* Dutton, 1975, 70 pages.

Sleator, William. *The Boy Who Reversed Himself.* Dutton, 1986, 167 pages.

Sleator, William. *Fingers.* Atheneum, 1983, 197 pages.

Sleator, William. *Into the Dream.* Dutton, 1979, 147 pages.

Sleator, William. *Run.* Dutton, 1973, 111 pages.

Sleator, William. *Singularity.* Dutton, 1985, 170 pages.

Sleator, William. *Strange Attractors.* Dutton, 1990, 169 pages.

Smith, K. *Skeeter.* Houghton Mifflin, 1989, 208 pages.

Smith, R. *The Squeaky Wheel.* Delacorte, 1990, 182 pages.

Snyder, Zilpha Keatley. *Libby On Wednesday.* Delacorte Press, 1990, 196 pages.

Sonnenmark, Laura A. *Something's Rotten In the State of Maryland.* Scholastic Inc., 1990, 165 pages.

Soto, Gary. *Taking Sides.* Harcourt Brace Jovanovich, 1991, 138 pages.

Spinelli, Jerry. *Maniac Magee.* Little, Brown, 1990, 184 pages.

Spinelli, Jerry. *Night of the Whale.* Dell, 1988.

Spinelli, Jerry. *There's a Girl In My Hammerlock.* Simon and Schuster, 1991, 199 pages.

Spinelli, Jerry. *Who Put That Hair In My Toothbrush?* Little, Brown, 1984, 220 pages.

Stine, R.L. *The Babysitter II.* Scholastic Inc., 1991, 176 pages.

Stine, R.L. *Beach House.* Scholastic Inc., 1992, 224 pages.

Stine, R.L. *Blind Date.* Scholastic Inc., 1986.

Stine, R.L. *Broken Date.* Archway, 1991, 224 pages.

Stine, R.L. *Curtains.* Archway, 1990, 160 pages.

Stine, R.L. *The Girlfriend.* Scholastic Inc., 1991, 176 pages.

Stine, R.L. *The Overnight.* Archway, 1991.

Stine, R.L. *The Sleepwalker.* Archway, 1991, 160 pages.

Stine, R.L. *The Snowman.* Scholastic Inc., 1991.

Strasser, Todd. *The Accident.* Delacorte Press, 1988, 178 pages.

Talbert, Marc. *Pillow of Clouds.* Dial Books, 1991, 204 pages.

Taylor, John Robert. *Hairline Cracks.* Dutton, 1988, 137 pages.

Taylor, Theodore. *Sniper.* Harcourt Brace Jovanovich, 1989, 226 pages.

Taylor, Theodore. *The Weirdo.* Harcourt Brace Jovanovich, 1991, 289 pages.

Thessman, Jean. *The Rain Catchers.* Houghton Mifflin, 1991, 182 pages.

Vail, Rachel. *Wonder.* Orchard Books, 1991, 122 pages.

Voigt, Cynthia. *Come a Stranger.* Atheneum, 1986, 190 pages.

Voigt, Cynthia. *The Vandemark Mummy.* Atheneum, 1991, 234 pages.

Wallace, Bill. *Danger In Quicksand Swamp.* Holiday House, 1989, 181 pages.

Westall, Robert. *Fathom Five.* Greenwillow Books, 1979, 242 pages.

Whelan, Gloria. *The Secret Keeper.* Knopf, 1990, 186 pages.

Williams-Garcia, Rita. *Fast Talk On a Slow Track.* Dutton, 1991, 182 pages.

Windsor, Patricia. *The Christmas Killer.* Scholastic Inc., 1991, 263 pages.

Wisler, G. Clifton. *The Mind Trap.* Dutton, 1990, 118 pages.

Wisler, G. Clifton. *Red Cap.* Dutton, 1991, 160 pages.

Wojciechowski, Susan. *And the Other Gold.* Orchard Books, 1987, 151 pages.

Wolff, Virginia. *The Mozart Season.* Henry Holt and Co., 1991, 249 pages.

Wood, Phyllis Anderson. *The Revolving Door Stops Here.* Cobblehill Books, 1990, 187 pages.

Wrede, Patricia C. *Dealing with Dragons.* Harcourt Brace Jovanovich, 1990, 212 pages.

Wright, Betty Ren. *The Scariest Night.* Holiday House, 1991, 166 pages.

Yolen, Jane. *The Dragon's Boy.* Harper and Row, 1990, 120 pages.

Zindel, Paul. *The Pigman.* Harper and Row, 1968, 182 pages.

Zindel, Paul. *The Pigman's Legacy.* Harper and Row, 1980, 183 pages.

THE ACCIDENT
Todd Strasser

1. Who is the only survivor of the crash?
   A. Bobby
   B. Randy
   C. Jason

2. Why didn't Matt go with the group when they left the party?
   A. he was barfing
   B. he was angry with Chris
   C. Karen refused to go with him

3. What do Bobby's parents donate to the school in memory of Bobby?
   A. swimming pool
   B. field house
   C. computer lab

4. Who was driving the truck when the accident occurred?
   A. Chris
   B. Bobby
   C. Jason

5. Who saw whom get into the driver's seat?
   A. Mrs. Walsh
   B. Matt
   C. Casey

6. What office is Bobby's uncle running for?
   A. Mayor
   B. Governor
   C. District Attorney

7. What is in the envelope that is slipped under Matt's door?
   A. hush money
   B. threat to mind his own business
   C. blood alcohol levels of the victims

8. What is Jason given for keeping quiet?
   A. mustang
   B. motorcycle
   C. high school diploma

9. What is Lee given for keeping quiet?
   A. gold badge
   B. ten thousand dollars
   C. job working for the Stewarts

10. What race is Lee?
    A. black
    B. white
    C. hispanic

ALESSANDRA IN LOVE
Robert Kaplow

1. What does Alessandra turn her reports in on?
   A. wrapping paper
   B. butcher paper
   C. construction paper

2. What were people supposed to wear to the school dance?
   A. swim suits
   B. formals
   C. costumes

3. Who is Alessandra's favorite singer?
   A. Throb
   B. Sting
   C. Ice Cube

4. What do Wynn and Alessandra do on most of their dates?
   A. play board games
   B. fight
   C. eat

5. What instrument does Alessandra play?
   A. oboe
   B. violin
   C. flute

6. What does Alessandra always have with her?
   A. address book
   B. journal
   C. silver locket

7. Who is Alessandra's best friend?
   A. Debbie
   B. Wynn
   C. Melissa

8. How do Wynn and Alessandra feel about each other after the weekend in New York City?
   A. they love each other
   B. they hate each other
   C. they are just friends

9. What clue lets Alessandra know what really happened in the hotel room?
   A. scarf
   B. the smell of perfume
   C. bracelet

10. Where does Alessandra's mother send her to get over Wynn?
    A. beach
    B. mountains
    C. Europe

ALEX, WHO WON HIS WAR
Chester Aaron

1. What does Oliver turn over to Alex when he enlists?
   A. his pocket knife
   B. his dog, Shadow
   C. his paper route

2. What does Alex hide in an old oil drum?
   A. wallet
   B. bat
   C. gold

3. What do the two spies dress up as?
   A. women
   B. waiters
   C. mechanics

4. What does Hans teach Alex to do?
   A. sing German folk songs
   B. carve figures
   C. draw portraits

5. What is wrong with Tony?
   A. he is blind in one eye
   B. he only has two fingers on his right hand
   C. he only has one leg

6. Who do Hans and Dieter hold captive?
   A. Tony and Alex
   B. Clara and Rosie
   C. Tony and Clara

7. What division is Oliver in?
   A. 21st Seamen
   B. 49th Army
   C. 101st Airborne

8. What are Hans and Dieter supposed to do in New London?
   A. infiltrate army intelligence
   B. blow up the submarine factory
   C. capture a warship

9. Who rescues Alex and the old women?
   A. Tony
   B. Dieter
   C. Alex' brother

10. What do Hans and Dieter borrow from Alex?
    A. fishing boat
    B. clothes
    C. car

ALICE, IN RAPTURE, SORT OF
Phyllis Reynolds Naylor

1. What does Alice give Patrick for his birthday?
   A. a record album
   B. a wallet
   C. a miniature drum set

2. Why doesn't Alice want to have the girls over to spend the night?
   A. she doesn't have a mom
   B. she doesn't want them to meet her family
   C. she doesn't live in a nice home

3. Where is Alice's summer job?
   A. in a music store
   B. at the zoo
   C. in a shoe store

4. In order to become beautiful what does Alice do?
   A. cut her hair
   B. get a permanent
   C. dye her hair

5. What does Pamela want Mark to apologize for?
   A. telling a lie about her
   B. tripping her in the mud and laughing
   C. taking her bra

6. What does Patrick try to help Alice do?
   A. bake a cake
   B. sing on pitch
   C. swim

7. What is Elizabeth too embarrassed to do?
   A. hold hands in public
   B. blow her nose in front of boys
   C. eat in front of boys

8. What happened while Alice was babysitting Jimmy?
   A. Jimmy fell out of bed
   B. Jimmy choked and turned blue
   C. Jimmy burned his hand

9. Where does Alice's father take the three girls?
   A. to the beach
   B. to the mountains
   C. to the lake

10. What does Alice find in the attic?
    A. her parents' old love letters
    B. her mother's diary
    C. her father's army uniform

AMONG THE DOLLS
William Sleator

1. What does Vicky's mother break?
   A. her hand
   B. a rare vase
   C. the law

2. What is the father doll missing?
   A. an eye
   B. hands and feet
   C. a mouth

3. Who named the dolls?
   A. the dolls
   B. Vicky
   C. the manufacturer

4. What does Vicky add to the doll house?
   A. a table
   B. another doll
   C. dishes

5. What does Vicky find in the doll house that she had never noticed before?
   A. a picture on a wall
   B. a toy mouse
   C. a doorway upstairs

6. What does Vicky promise Ganglia if she will help her leave?
   A. let her have control of the other dolls
   B. take her out of the doll house
   C. put her bed in the toy room

7. What is in the doll house's attic?
   A. a doll house
   B. a secret closet
   C. a treasure chest

8. Who tells Vicky how to escape?
   A. Ganglia, the girl
   B. the father doll
   C. Dandaroo, the boy

9. What does Vicky have to put into the doll house in order to get home?
   A. a family
   B. herself
   C. a charm

10. What do the dolls want to do to Vicky?
    A. kill her
    B. make her their slave
    C. throw her out

AND THE OTHER, GOLD
Susan Wojciechowski

1. Where does Tracy hide to scare Patty?
   A. in Patty's locker
   B. in Patty's car
   C. in Patty's closet

2. What do Patty and Tracy try out for?
   A. basketball team
   B. school play
   C. cheerleading squad

3. What does Father Damian collect?
   A. strange hats
   B. old cars
   C. baseball cards

4. What do the seventh graders start carrying to school everyday after Patty's article comes out?
   A. weapons
   B. lunch boxes
   C. school jackets

5. What do the seventh graders do to Patty?
   A. toilet paper her house
   B. shoe polish her car
   C. spray her locker and books with perfume

6. What do the cast and crew give Father Damian?
   A. their picture
   B. a party
   C. a cowboy hat

7. Where is Patty's private office?
   A. hall closet
   B. basement
   C. back porch

8. What is Chris' favorite thing to do?
   A. eat ice cream
   B. build models
   C. tattle

9. What does Patty do that causes her and Tracy to start talking again?
   A. buy her a coke
   B. write about friendship in the school paper
   C. send her a card apologizing

10. What is in the thermos in the girls' bathroom?
    A. coffee
    B. liquor
    C. lemon juice

ANDRA
Louise Lawrence

1. What happened to Andra as a result of her brain graft?
   A. her eyes and hair changed colors
   B. she was able to understand animals
   C. she was unable to speak her native language

2. Where does Andra work?
   A. in the medical lab
   B. in the archives
   C. in the computer room

3. What does Syrd do well?
   A. sing
   B. fix things
   C. tell jokes

4. How old is Kiroyo?
   A. 22 years old
   B. over 300 years old
   C. over 1,000 years old

5. What does Andra steal from the museum?
   A. photo album
   B. record player
   C. guitar

6. Who is the spy?
   A. Lascaux
   B. Kiroyo
   C. Syrd

7. What does Andra do that is considered defiant?
   A. she grows her hair long
   B. she carries a weapon
   C. she gets a pet

8. Who does Andra live with?
   A. Lascaux and Kiroyo
   B. Shenlyn and Cromer
   C. Syrd and Daemon

9. What is destroyed by sabotage?
   A. Sub City Three
   B. several ships
   C. the computer room

10. Where is Andra's body found?
    A. at E.D.C.O.
    B. on the surface
    C. in Sub City One

ARE WE THERE YET?
Marjorie Sharmat

1. What does Ted use to record his trip to Dallas?
   A. tape recorder
   B. journal
   C. camera

2. What does Ted borrow from his Uncle that gets ruined?
   A. shirt
   B. hat
   C. car

3. What does Uncle Tony hate?
   A. the Dearing dog
   B. the Dearing maid
   C. the Dearing home

4. What does Mrs. Dearing give Ted a check for?
   A. 50 dollars
   B. 1,000 dollars
   C. 50,000 dollars

5. Who gives Ted advice on the phone?
   A. Delphine
   B. Beth Ann
   C. Laura

6. What does Heidi do at everyone's home?
   A. ride horses
   B. play pool
   C. swim

7. What does Ted believe older women like?
   A. glistening bodies
   B. a good listener
   C. good manners

8. Who is Ted supposed to meet on a blind date?
   A. Delphine
   B. Beth Ann
   C. Laura

9. What does Ted tell Delphine and Beth Ann at the barbecue?
   A. about his school
   B. about his vacation
   C. about his hobbies

10. What are Ted's aunt and uncle good at?
    A. offending people
    B. planning things
    C. not finishing what they start

ARE YOU IN THE HOUSE ALONE?
Richard Peck

1. How many obscene letters does Gail receive?
   A. 7
   B. 5
   C. 2

2. When Gail reports the letters and calls to the school counselor what does the counselor do?
   A. tell her she is making it up
   B. call the police
   C. tell her parents

3. Why does Gail go to New York City?
   A. to see her dad
   B. to run away from home
   C. to visit her aunt

4. Who rapes Gail?
   A. Steve
   B. Phil
   C. Coach

5. Where was Gail when she was attacked?
   A. the locker room at school
   B. home fixing dinner in the kitchen
   C. Mrs. Montgomery's house babysitting

6. What does the attacker hit Gail with?
   A. baseball bat
   B. fireplace poker
   C. lamp

7. What does the attacker do after he attacks Gail?
   A. threatens her on the phone
   B. asks her for a date
   C. sends her flowers

8. Who is Madam Malevich?
   A. very young crisis counselor
   B. star of the silent screen
   C. Gail's great aunt

9. Who is the attacker's second victim?
   A. Sonia
   B. Allison
   C. Madam Malevich

10. What happens to Gail's attacker?
    A. he mysteriously disappears
    B. he goes to prison
    C. he is found shot to death

THE BABYSITTER II
R.L. Stine

1. What does Eli have for pets?
   A. a snake
   B. four pink rats
   C. three tarantulas

2. What did Eli build from a kit?
   A. computer and phone
   B. radio and model plane
   C. microwave and walkman

3. What does Jenny find in her handbag?
   A. dead tarantula
   B. a threatening note
   C. the tape of her session

4. What does Dr. Schindler think about the phone calls Jenny is getting?
   A. she's in real danger
   B. she imagined them
   C. someone is playing a joke on her

5. How did Claire get hurt?
   A. poisoned by a spider bite
   B. broke her neck in a wreck
   C. fell down the stairs

6. Who does Jenny think is trying to scare her?
   A. Chuck
   B. Dr. Schindler
   C. Cal

7. What does Eli do that surprises everyone?
   A. refuses to stay with Jenny
   B. hurts Claire
   C. hugs and kisses Jenny

8. Who was really scaring Jenny?
   A. Mr. Hagan
   B. Miss Gurney
   C. Eli

9. What did Miss Gurney do to Cal?
   A. push him over the edge of the rock quarry
   B. hit him with a lead pipe
   C. demand that he leave

10. What did Miss Gurney try to do to Jenny?
    A. drown her
    B. shoot her
    C. stab her

BEACH HOUSE
R.L.Stine

1. Why does Buddy kill Maria, Amy, Ronnie and Stuart?
   A. they told his girl he was dating someone else
   B. they stole his surfboard
   C. they made fun of him

2. What joke do Ronnie and Stuart play on Buddy?
   A. they take off his pants in the ocean
   B. they scare him in the beach house
   C. they leave him tied up on the beach

3. How does Buddy kill Amy?
   A. drown her in the tide
   B. strangle her with a scarf
   C. hit her with drift wood

4. What does Ashley play when she's at Brad's house?
   A. horse shoes
   B. tennis
   C. chess

5. Why is Ashley upset with Ross?
   A. he doesn't ever want to do anything
   B. he stood her up
   C. he is extremely jealous

6. What two people are the same?
   A. Ronnie and Brad
   B. Buddy and Brad
   C. Amy and Mary

7. Who survives Buddy's murder attempt?
   A. Ronnie
   B. Brad
   C. Maria

8. Who dies in the beach house fire?
   A. Stuart
   B. Mary
   C. Amy

9. When does this story take place?
   A. 1950's and 1980's
   B. 1990's and 2010's
   C. 1880's and 1920's

10. What is the secret of the beach house?
    A. it is built on a time warp
    B. there is no way out once entered
    C. it is haunted by the spirits of the dead

BEING OF TWO MINDS
Pamela F. Service

1. Who wakes up Connie's parents in the early morning hours?
   A. president of America
   B. Rudy's parents
   C. CIA

2. Who is Wolfie?
   A. Rudy's tutor
   B. Rudy's doctor
   C. Rudy's uncle

3. What do Rudy and Connie learn from visiting each others' minds over the years?
   A. another language
   B. how to read thoughts
   C. how the other's food tastes

4. Where do Rudy and Connie actually meet and talk face to face for the first time?
   A. White House
   B. Chicago
   C. Thulgaria

5. What happened to Connie's luggage?
   A. it was lost
   B. it was stolen
   C. it was blown up

6. How was Wolfie injured?
   A. he was shot
   B. he was run down
   C. he was shoved over a cliff

7. Where is Rudy being held?
   A. convent
   B. dungeon
   C. castle

8. What does Connie meet on the path in the woods?
   A. wolf
   B. dog
   C. bear

9. Who was in on the plot to get rid of Rudy?
   A. his uncle
   B. his sister
   C. his tutor

10. What did Gustav like to build?
    A. secret passages
    B. bridges
    C. garden terraces

BINGO BROWN, GYPSY LOVER
Betsy Byars

1. What does Bingo say is growing too fast?
   A. his feet
   B. his ears
   C. his arms

2. Who does Boots call for Christmas?
   A. Melissa
   B. Boots
   C. Billy

3. Why does Bingo's mother name him Bingo?
   A. it's what the doctor said when he was born
   B. he was born on bingo night
   C. it was his grandfather's name

4. What does Billy Wentworth accidentally give Cici for Christmas?
   A. GI Joe
   B. Brute aftershave
   C. belt buckle

5. What does Bingo buy for Melissa for Christmas?
   A. perfume
   B. poetry book
   C. gold earrings

6. What does Melissa make Bingo for Christmas?
   A. sweater
   B. notebook holder
   C. cookies

7. Why is Bingo's mother in the hospital?
   A. she broke her leg
   B. she has food poisoning
   C. to have a baby

8. How are the babies sent home from the hospital?
   A. in blue or pink blankets
   B. in red stockings
   C. in red knit caps

9. Why does Boots call Bingo on the phone?
   A. to read Gypsy Lover to him
   B. to ask for the homework assignment
   C. to ask for a date to go skating

10. What does Bingo give his mother for Christmas?
    A. fudge
    B. to clean house for a month
    C. he agrees to babysit for one month

597186

BLIND DATE
R.L. Stine

1. What happened to Kerry's locker?
   A. red paint was poured inside
   B. contents were stolen
   C. stink bomb was thrown in

2. What happened at the dance?
   A. Kerry's date didn't show up
   B. Kerry's car was vandalized
   C. Kerry spilled punch on his date

3. Where did Donald escape from?
   A. a mental institution
   B. the state prison
   C. his kidnappers

4. What is Kerry's father?
   A. a doctor
   B. a policeman
   C. a telephone repairman

5. What happens after Kerry breaks Sal's leg?
   A. he takes Sal's place on the team
   B. he quits the team
   C. he is kicked off the team

6. What happened a year ago that Kerry can't remember?
   A. his mother drowned trying to save him
   B. he paralyzed his best friend in a ball game
   C. he killed Donald's girl in an accident

7. Why is Donald taken away?
   A. he tried to kill Kerry
   B. he is a drug addict
   C. he is insane

8. Why does Donald escape?
   A. to kill Kerry
   B. to kill Mandy
   C. to save Kerry

9. What does Mandy put on Kerry's head?
   A. a blindfold
   B. a stuffed moose head
   C. a mask

10. What does Mandy do with the wooden mallet?
    A. break the dishes
    B. bang on the wall
    C. break Kerry's toes

BLINDFOLD
Sandra McCuaig

1. Where does Sally first see Joel and Benji?
   A. school football game
   B. school dance
   C. school debating contest

2. What does Sally do to Joel before she ever meets him?
   A. trips him
   B. scares him
   C. kisses him

3. What did Sally's father do for a living?
   A. horse racing bookie
   B. hit man for the mob
   C. professional thief

4. What do Joel and Benji win at the fair?
   A. stuffed bear
   B. ham
   C. T-shirt

5. What is Sally's cat's name?
   A. Kitten
   B. Cat
   C. Miaow

6. What do Benji and Joel call Sally?
   A. Carrot
   B. Flame
   C. Red

7. What do Sally and Kate give Joel for his birthday?
   A. hat
   B. book
   C. sunglasses

8. Where do Joel and Benji jump from?
   A. water tower
   B. cliff
   C. high rise building

9. What does Dr. Jago buy with Sally's help?
   A. new suit
   B. new office furniture
   C. new car

10. What does Mrs. Goldstein find in Benji's room?
    A. fake horoscope
    B. bad report card
    C. suicide note

A BLOSSOM PROMISE

Betsy Byars

1. What does Pap almost do four times as a child?
    A. drown
    B. get snake bit
    C. get trampled by a steer

2. Why is Junior's trip to see Mary postponed?
    A. Junior gets sick
    B. creek has flooded its banks
    C. Mary breaks her leg

3. What does Michael's mother not let Vern and Michael have?
    A. a paddle
    B. an old sheet
    C. some rope

4. What was the name of the raft?
    A. the Dutchess
    B. the Queen
    C. the Lady

5. What happened to Dump?
    A. he was shot
    B. he was run over
    C. he was snake bit

6. How did Michael and Vern get out of the creek?
    A. by swimming
    B. by holding on to vines
    C. by grabbing a fallen tree

7. What was Pap doing at the creek?
    A. roping Michael and Vern
    B. fishing with Maggie
    C. swimming with Junior

8. What was wrong with Pap?
    A. he was senile
    B. he was upset because he got lost
    C. he had a heart attack

9. What do Ralphie and Maggie smuggle into Pap's hospital room?
    A. pizza
    B. Mud
    C. beer

10. What does Vickie say the Blossoms will do in the fall?
    A. enter rodeos
    B. start a riding school
    C. add a new member to the family

THE BORNING ROOM
Paul Fleischman

1. What does Hattie say causes babies?
   A. standing outside under a full moon
   B. putting a horseshoe under the bed
   C. swallowing watermelon seeds

2. Who is the runaway slave?
   A. Cora
   B. Ada
   C. Clement

3. Who does Georgina tell about helping the slave?
   A. no one
   B. Hattie
   C. Ada

4. What is the sign that a baby will die?
   A. the cows won't give milk
   B. a bird gets into the house
   C. a broken jar

5. Who does Georgina get to help deliver her mother's baby?
   A. Mrs. Reedy
   B. Mrs. Radtke
   C. Cora

6. Where does Grandfather worship on Sundays?
   A. at the schoolhouse
   B. in the field
   C. at the Methodist church

7. Who was sent for just before Grandfather died?
   A. preacher
   B. doctor
   C. painter

8. What killed Georgina's mother?
   A. fall off a ladder
   B. chloroform
   C. snake bite

9. What does Mr. Bock blow down Zeb's throat when he is sick?
   A. eggshells
   B. broth
   C. air

10. What do people who come to see grandfather on his deathbed do?
    A. lecture him on hell
    B. thank him for all he's done
    C. hold his hand and comfort him

THE BOY WHO LOST HIS FACE
Louis Sachar

1. What does David do to Mrs. Bayfield while his friends steal her cane?
   A. hold her down
   B. break her window
   C. shoot the bird at her

2. What do Larry and David help carry to Mo's house?
   A. a doghouse
   B. a wrecked bicycle
   C. a science project

3. Who is given the name, 'The Three Stooges'?
   A. Larry, Mo, and David
   B. David, Scott, and Mo
   C. Roger, Randy, and Scott

4. What does Larry tell David to do in order to break the curse?
   A. say the Gettysburg address backwards
   B. pour lemonade on his head
   C. wear garlic while showering

5. Who gets the cane from Roger?
   A. David
   B. Larry
   C. Tori

6. What does Mrs. Bayfield have all over her walls?
   A. photographs
   B. masks
   C. paintings

7. What does Mrs. Bayfield tell David to do to remove the curse?
   A. give her his face for a trophy
   B. touch her bloomers
   C. drink yellow liquid and kiss Tori

8. Who is Mrs. Bayfield?
   A. Tori's grandmother
   B. Tori's great aunt
   C. Tori's neighbor

9. Who has been David's best friend since second grade?
   A. Scott
   B. Randy
   C. Larry

10. What does Mrs. Bayfield say David has?
    A. the soul of a poet
    B. the feet of a dancer
    C. the hands of a pianist

THE BOY WHO OWNED THE SCHOOL
Gary Paulsen

1. What does Jacob believe will happen if he is noticed?
    A. he will become popular
    B. he will go to jail
    C. bad things

2. What does Jacob's sister call him?
    A. Buttwad
    B. Potato Head
    C. Ding Bat

3. What do Jacob's parents do a lot of?
    A. drinking
    B. swearing
    C. gambling

4. What happened to Jacob in gym class?
    A. he won the hoop game
    B. he ran over and stepped on Maria
    C. no one picked him for their team

5. What is Jacob's favorite class?
    A. math
    B. gym
    C. industrial arts

6. What bad thing happens in Jacob's day dream?
    A. he is hit by a bus
    B. his necktie is caught in the locker door
    C. Maria laughs at him

7. What is Jacob's role in the school play
    A. be a munchkin
    B. build the set
    C. run the fog machine

8. Why does everyone leave before the play is over?
    A. the play is awful
    B. they think the school is on fire
    C. a storm is on the way

9. What does Maria agree to do with Jacob?
    A. go on a date
    B. repair the fog machine
    C. practice her lines

10. What does Maria call Jacob?
    A. a winner
    B. a clutz
    C. a geek

THE BOY WHO REVERSED HIMSELF
William Sleator

1. Where does Omar take Laura?
   A. 4th dimension
   B. 3rd dimension
   C. 2nd dimension

2. What reversed food does Laura like to eat?
   A. peanut butter
   B. ketchup
   C. pickles

3. Where do Laura and Pete get trapped?
   A. school roof
   B. locker room
   C. broom closet

4. What can not be done in 4 space?
   A. jump
   B. tie a knot
   C. have an echo

5. What can you do in 4 space that you can't do in 3 space?
   A. float
   B. walk on water
   C. see through each other

6. How do Laura and Pete understand the creatures?
   A. through signals
   B. through an interpreter
   C. through telepathy

7. Where do the creatures keep Laura and Pete?
   A. in a cage
   B. in a cave
   C. in a locked room

8. What does Ramoom give to Laura and Pete?
   A. a ball
   B. a dog
   C. eye glasses

9. What does Ramoom want Pete to find his way out of?
   A. the 4th dimension
   B. a maze
   C. a locked cage

10. What is Omar in training to be?
    A. a champion wrestler
    B. guardian of the 2nd dimension
    C. the emperor of Iran

THE BRAVE
Robert Lypsyte

1. What does Sonny become for Stick?
   A. his mule
   B. his bodyguard
   C. his press agent

2. Where does Stick hide his shotgun and knife?
   A. inside his coat
   B. inside his walking stick
   C. inside his fake leg

3. Why is Sonny a hero in prison?
   A. he decked the guard
   B. he smuggled cocaine in
   C. the guards couldn't break him

4. What secret society does Jake say Sonny will soon be a part of?
   A. Shooting Arrows
   B. Running Braves
   C. True Tongues

5. How does Sonny pay for his boxing lessons?
   A. by making pizza deliveries
   B. by selling crack
   C. by cleaning the gym

6. Who shoots Alfred Brooks?
   A. Mo
   B. Chubs
   C. Stick

7. Why is Sonny disqualified from the tournament?
   A. he had fought for money before
   B. he had taken steroids
   C. he threw illegal punches

8. What does Sonny's mother do for a living?
   A. fly commercial planes
   B. teach Indian dances
   C. make jewelry

9. What is Sonny's hobby?
   A. singing
   B. drawing
   C. fishing

10. Who is Sonny's assistant trainer?
    A. Brooks
    B. Martin
    C. Johnson

BREAKING OUT
Barthe De Clement

1. What does Jerry wake up Matt in the middle of the night to tell him?
   A. he's running away
   B. his house is on fire
   C. Matt's car is being stolen

2. What does Jerry write about in his autobiography?
   A. the divorce
   B. his dad's arrest
   C. Willard and the restaurant

3. What does Mrs. Castle say Jerry's a natural at?
   A. acting
   B. writing
   C. sports

4. What does security do to Jerry and his mother when they go to see his father at the prison?
   A. have them leave their belongings
   B. stamp their hands
   C. give them badges

5. What does Russell tell Mrs. Castle?
   A. Jerry's dad's in prison
   B. Jerry can't act
   C. Jerry knows all about stealing

6. Who does Jerry imitate in Mrs. Castle's class?
   A. his father singing
   B. his p.e. teacher dancing
   C. a monkey eating a banana

7. What kind of commercial is Jerry in?
   A. food
   B. clothes
   C. car

8. Where does Willard make Jerry work?
   A. in his office
   B. in his restaurant
   C. in the yard

9. Who does Jerry say taught him to act?
   A. his father
   B. his mother
   C. the TV

10. How does Grace get even with Jenson at the dance?
    A. she pours punch on his head
    B. she refuses to dance with him
    C. she slaps him

BROKEN DATE
R.L. Stine

1. What does Jamie see Tom do
   A. rob a jewelry store and kill the manager
   B. commit a hit and run accident
   C. strangle a waitress

2. What does Jamie think she did at the school dance?
   A. slap Tom in the face
   B. stab Tom with a pick
   C. throw coke in Tom's face

3. What is in the package Tom leaves for Jamie the morning after the dance?
   A. gold loop earrings
   B. a bomb
   C. money

4. What does the voice on the phone say?
   A. meet me behind the school
   B. I'm really sorry
   C. nothing

5. What happens to Tom's dad?
   A. he loses his job
   B. he is stuck at the airport
   C. he is in an accident upstate

6. What does Tom tell Jamie in the letter he leaves for her?
   A. he's guilty
   B. he's innocent
   C. we all act crazy

7. What does Jamie leave in the jewelry store?
   A. her wallet
   B. her purse
   C. her raincoat

8. What does Okie Farnum plan to do to Tom and Jamie?
   A. run them over with the van
   B. smother them with a pillow
   C. drown them in a tub

9. Why does Jamie think Okie is Tom in the jewelry store?
   A. Okie has on the same shirt
   B. Okie has the same hair
   C. Okie has the same walk

10. How is Tom able to follow Okie's van?
    A. in his car
    B. riding on the back of the van
    C. on horseback

BROTHERS OF THE HEART
Joan W. Blos

1. Where does Shem's family move to?
   A. farm
   B. ocean
   C. town

2. What is wrong with Shem's father?
   A. he caught the ager
   B. he cut his leg off
   C. he broke his arm

3. What job does Shem get paid $12 to do?
   A. take money to another bank
   B. work on the railroad
   C. shoeing horses

4. What job does Shem get after he runs away?
   A. bank teller
   B. clerk position
   C. cow hand

5. What does Mary Goodhue teach Shem to use?
   A. bow and arrow
   B. skinning knife
   C. snowshoes

6. Who does Shem's father send for in a letter?
   A. a bride
   B. Sophy
   C. a teacher

7. Who does Sophy marry?
   A. Shem
   B. Zozep
   C. Uncle Jack

8. How does Shem get back to Detroit after burying Mary Goodhue?
   A. train
   B. canoe
   C. horse

9. What does Shem leave in the cabin when he returns to Detroit?
   A. his boots
   B. his ledger
   C. his buckskin shirt

10. Of the people who went with Shem to trade for furs, who came back alive?
    A. Zozep
    B. Beaubien
    C. Good Pierre

BUFFALO BRENDA
Jill Pinkwater

1. What is Brenda's first article in the school paper about?
   A. the Buffalo football team
   B. school spirit
   C. popularity breeds contempt

2. What causes the newspaper staff to be fired?
   A. students rate the teachers article
   B. misuse of school money
   C. vandalism of the newspaper equipment

3. What do the students do after they are kicked off the school paper?
   A. start an underground paper
   B. spray paint the principal's car
   C. trash the newspaper office

4. What is being served in the school cafeteria?
   A. soy burgers
   B. horse meat
   C. veggie burgers

5. What do the students have an assembly for?
   A. lecture on the evils of drugs
   B. pep rally for the big game
   C. funeral for some horses

6. How does Brenda's grandfather tame the bison?
   A. by singing to him
   B. by feeding him oatmeal raisin cookies
   C. by riding him until he gives up

7. Where does the bison stay at first?
   A. in Brenda's backyard
   B. in the zoo
   C. in a garage

8. What does Brenda name the bison?
   A. Sharon
   B. Florence
   C. India

9. What is wrong with the bison?
   A. it is having a baby
   B. it ate bad hay
   C. it hurt its leg

10. Where does the bison end up living?
    A. on a wildlife refuge
    B. in the local zoo
    C. on the football field

BUNKHOUSE JOURNAL
Diane Johnston Hamm

1. Where is Sandy from?
   A. Los Angeles
   B. New York
   C. Denver

2. What does Karen make for Sandy that he treasures?
   A. mittens
   B. hat
   C. coat

3. What is Sandy's father's problem?
   A. he's an alcoholic
   B. he is a drug addict
   C. he's abusive

4. What does Sandy buy for Joanna?
   A. boots
   B. violin strings
   C. cow

5. Who does not want to date Sandy?
   A. Joanna
   B. Christine
   C. Karen

6. Why is Karen required to stay on the couch?
   A. she broke her foot
   B. she is having a baby
   C. she has a concussion

7. What does Martha tell Sandy in her letter?
   A. that she is pregnant
   B. his father is dead
   C. that Sandy should come live with her

8. Who is poor?
   A. Karen
   B. Joanna
   C. Christine

9. What does Karen give to Sandy that had belonged to his mother?
   A. necklace
   B. photograph
   C. Bible

10. What does Sandy decide to do in the fall?
    A. go to college
    B. get married
    C. buy land

CAGES
Peg Kehret

1. What crime does Kit commit?
   A. breaking and entering
   B. assault
   C. shoplifting

2. What does Kit's stepfather call her?
   A. an animal
   B. dumpling
   C. peaches

3. What is Kit's stepfather's problem?
   A. alcohol
   B. his temper
   C. fear of failing

4. In speech class what does Kit give a speech about?
   A. drugs
   B. shoplifting
   C. teenage pregnancy

5. Who does Kit visit in the hospital?
   A. her best friend
   B. her grandfather
   C. her mother

6. What instrument does the man at the humane society play for the animals?
   A. flute
   B. harmonica
   C. guitar

7. What award does Kit get at the school assembly?
   A. Spanish award
   B. best all around athlete
   C. scholarship

8. What part does Kit have in the school play?
   A. making the scenery
   B. making the posters
   C. the leading lady

9. How does Kit's stepfather break his arm?
   A. driving drunk
   B. falling off a ladder
   C. fighting

10. What is Kit's job at the humane society?
    A. to socialize the dogs
    B. to feed the dogs
    C. to clean out the cages

CAN YOU SUE YOUR PARENTS FOR MALPRACTICE?
Paula Danziger

1. What does Lauren do that her father told her not to do?
    A. stay out past midnight
    B. go out with Zack
    C. pierce her ears

2. What does Lauren give to Linda?
    A. her training bra
    B. her purple sweater
    C. her stuffed bear

3. What does Lauren's mother want to do?
    A. be on a game show
    B. win the lottery
    C. have a baby

4. What kind of job does Lauren's mother get?
    A. midwife
    B. substitute teacher
    C. zoo keeper

5. What does Bonnie's mother give to Lauren?
    A. a loan
    B. a puppy
    C. gold hoop earrings

6. Why do Zack's parents get a divorce?
    A. because of a job
    B. because of child abuse
    C. because of an affair

7. Why is Lauren's father angry with Melissa?
    A. she dropped out of college
    B. she is pregnant
    C. she moves in with Mike

8. What does Zack hate?
    A. spinach
    B. large parties
    C. reading

9. What are people betting on?
    A. how long Zack and Lauren will stay together
    B. whether Mr. Matthews will be fired
    C. when Lauren's sister will be allowed to come home

10. What do Lauren and Zack do in his bedroom just before they start to make out?
    A. set the timer
    B. lock the door
    C. brush their teeth

A CANDIDATE FOR MURDER

Joan Lowery Nixon

1. What does Mark accuse Cary of?
   A. taking his film
   B. dating another boy
   C. crashing his party

2. Who keeps calling Cary to warn her about getting hurt?
   A. Dexter
   B. Nora
   C. Justin

3. What accident does Cary's dad want to investigate?
   A. a bridge collapsing
   B. a train derailing
   C. a car going over a cliff

4. What gets vandalized with blue paint?
   A. Cary's car
   B. campaign office
   C. Cary's home

5. Why are Cary and Justin arrested on their way home from the Halloween dance?
   A. disorderly conduct
   B. drinking while driving
   C. possession of drugs

6. Who was run down by a car?
   A. Cary
   B. Justin
   C. Cindy

7. Who helps Cary get information on people?
   A. Sally Jo
   B. Justin
   C. Mark

8. Where is Cary when the gunman tries to kill her?
   A. at the drug store
   B. in the parking lot
   C. at a banquet

9. What does Cary hear that puts her life in danger?
   A. a bribe being accepted
   B. talk about a murder
   C. how drugs are being smuggled

10. Who is Dexter?
    A. the butler
    B. a bodyguard
    C. Cary's boyfriend

CANYONS
Gary Paulsen

1. How does Brennan make money?
   A. babysitting
   B. throwing newspapers
   C. mowing lawns

2. What does Coyote Runs put on his arrows?
   A. tobacco
   B. oil
   C. salt

3. Why does Brennan run?
   A. for the joy of running
   B. to win a race
   C. to escape the police

4. Where does Bill take Brennan and his mother?
   A. ice skating
   B. camping
   C. to work

5. What does Coyote Runs want to shoot on the raid?
   A. snakes
   B. deer
   C. bluebellies

6. What did Coyote Runs spit into?
   A. a can
   B. a horse's mouth
   C. the ground

7. What did Brennan bring to his biology teacher each day?
   A. his homework
   B. an apple
   C. different beetles

8. Who was chasing Brennan?
   A. a killer
   B. a rescue party
   C. a ghost

9. Where did Brennan leave the skull?
   A. on a square rock
   B. under a tree
   C. in a cave

10. Where did Brennan get water in the desert?
    A. Yucca cactus
    B. an oasis
    C. an underground spring

CAUGHT IN THE ACT
Joan Lowery Nixon

1. What does Mr. Crandon whisper to all the families when they come to see the orphans?
   A. Mike saved a lady's ring from thieves
   B. Frances is a girl
   C. Mike is a thief

2. What happened to Mike the first night at the Friedrich's?
   A. he is whipped
   B. he is sent to bed without supper
   C. he gets in a fight with Gunter

3. What does Reuben like to do?
   A. read poetry
   B. play the harmonica
   C. sing

4. What does Gunter accuse Mike of?
   A. not doing his chores
   B. stealing a gold watch
   C. hitting him

5. What is Mike not allowed to do?
   A. go to church
   B. write his mother
   C. go to school

6. What does Mike accuse Mr. Friedrich of?
   A. beating Mrs. Friedrich
   B. killing Reuben
   C. stealing money

7. Who was Ulrich?
   A. a runaway slave
   B. the old hired help
   C. Mr. Friedrich's son

8. Why does Mike run away?
   A. to find Frances
   B. to find Reuben
   C. to find a new home

9. What does Mike find behind the toolbox in the barn?
   A. Reuben's book
   B. blood
   C. the axe

10. What was buried in the woods?
    A. coins from Germany
    B. Reuben's body
    C. the murder weapon

CHECKING ON THE MOON
Jenny Davis

1. What does Cab's stepfather do?
   A. pianist
   B. golf pro
   C. astronaut

2. What does Grandmother call Cranston Oliver?
   A. Beethoven
   B. Shakespeare
   C. Einstein

3. What class does Cab take at the library?
   A. reading and writing
   B. pottery
   C. self defense

4. What does Tracy believe she's going to be when she grows up?
   A. a failure
   B. great
   C. rich

5. What is Sally's baby's name?
   A. Wonder
   B. Rainbow
   C. Marvel

6. What was Jessica a victim of?
   A. a mugging
   B. a kidnapping
   C. a rape

7. How did Tracy and Cab get skinned up?
   A. jumping from a moving train
   B. falling off the chimney
   C. chasing a mugger

8. What is Bill's big announcement at the restaurant?
   A. he's getting married
   B. he's quitting college
   C. he's not moving to Wisconsin

9. What does Washco do to stop crime?
   A. put bars on windows
   B. hold a vigil
   C. carry guns

10. Where do Cab's parents tell her she will live next year?
    A. Rome, Italy
    B. Brussels, Belgium
    C. Paris, France

CHILD OF THE AIR
Grace Chetwin

1. Who does Mylanfyndra get when Grandpa falls ill?
   A. Toova
   B. Ebbwe
   C. Ryke

2. What do the town people do with dead bodies?
   A. send them off the cliff
   B. burn them
   C. wrap them in large leaves and bury them

3. What do Mylanfyndra and Brevan become after Grandpa dies?
   A. geth
   B. vine tenders
   C. shepherds

4. What do Brevan and Mylanfyndra do when they go to the podilithra at night?
   A. tell stories
   B. fly
   C. play games

5. Where are Brevan and Mylanfyndra put when they are found guilty of being evil?
   A. underground cave
   B. jail
   C. cage for thieves

6. Who set Brevan and Mylanfyndra free?
   A. Toova
   B. Ebbwe
   C. Krels

7. Who brings Brevan and Mylanfyndra to their new home in Telfyra?
   A. Toova
   B. Calen
   C. Yoleyna

8. What is Brevan's favorite subject?
   A. skytrailing
   B. mapmaking
   C. languages

9. Where do Brevan and Mylanfyndra live in Telfyra?
   A. in the dormitories
   B. with Yoleyna
   C. with their real parents

10. What do Mylanfyndra and Yoleyna find is wrong with Ebbwe?
    A. she has a broken leg
    B. she has been beaten
    C. she has a concussion

CHILDREN OF THE RIVER
Linda Crew

1. How does Sundara's family support themselves?
   A. harvest crops by hand
   B. do janitor work
   C. do road construction work

2. What does Jonathan do to Ravy that is not acceptable?
   A. talk to him alone
   B. touch Ravy on the head
   C. give him American clothes

3. Where is Sundara from?
   A. Phnom Penh
   B. Chicago
   C. Peking

4. Where does Sundara last see her father?
   A. in a hotel
   B. at the airport
   C. at home

5. Where do Jonathan's parents take Sundara?
   A. to a museum
   B. to the park
   C. sailing

6. What is Jonathan writing a school report on?
   A. the king of England
   B. World War II
   C. Cambodia

7. What does Sundara want to become?
   A. a doctor
   B. a teacher
   C. a singer

8. Why does Sundara go to see Dr. McKennon?
   A. to deliver a message
   B. to learn English
   C. to teach him Khmer language

9. Why is Jonathan in the hospital?
   A. broken leg
   B. concussion
   C. high fever

10. What does Sundara do with her Aunt Soka's dead baby?
    A. bury it
    B. throw it overboard
    C. cremate it

THE CHOCOLATE WAR
Robert Cormier

1. What did Archie tell Goober to do with the screwdriver?
   A. fix Archie's bicycle
   B. rig the fire alarm
   C. unscrew everything in Brother Eugene's room

2. What did Brother Leon say to Bailey after he slapped him?
   A. Why do you cheat?
   B. Only bullies fight
   C. Go to the office

3. What does Emile want to get from Archie?
   A. a photograph
   B. the black box
   C. money

4. Who is the secretary of the Vigils?
   A. Archie
   B. Obie
   C. Carter

5. What do the students do every time Brother Jacques says the word, 'environment'?
   A. whistle
   B. jump three times
   C. dance a jig

6. What happened to Brother Eugene?
   A. he quit
   B. he had a nervous breakdown
   C. he was fired

7. What does Goober tell Jerry he's going to do?
   A. beat up Archie
   B. tell Brother Leon about his assignment
   C. quit the football team

8. At the beginning of the chocolate sale why does Jerry refuse to sell the chocolate?
   A. he didn't want to
   B. the Vigils told him not to
   C. his parents wouldn't let him

9. What is in the black box?
   A. marbles
   B. money from the chocolate sale
   C. the assignments

10. Who do the students buy tickets to see box?
    A. Emile and Jerry
    B. Archie and Obie
    C. Archie and Emile

THE CHRISTMAS KILLER
Patricia Windsor

1. Who does Jerram tell Rose to tell about her dreams?
   A. Chief Henning
   B. Detective O'Hara
   C. Mackey

2. Where is the skeleton found?
   A. junk yard
   B. basement
   C. farm

3. Where was Cindy's body found?
   A. caves
   B. lake
   C. ditch

4. What does the Christmas killer leave on his victims?
   A. red scarf
   B. red plastic poinsettia
   C. red stocking

5. Who does Rose like?
   A. Jerram
   B. Gregory
   C. Daniel

6. When did Rose's mother say Rose died and came back to life?
   A. when she was a baby
   B. before she was born
   C. when she was five

7. What does Muriel teach Rose?
   A. piano
   B. tumbling
   C. dance

8. Who is the Christmas killer?
   A. Gregory
   B. Muriel's twin brother
   C. Mackey

9. Who saved Rose from the killer?
   A. Wallace
   B. Daniel
   C. Jerram

10. What did the killer's sister blame him for as a child?
    A. killing a puppy
    B. stealing her dolls
    C. cutting up pictures of her girlfriends

CLAY MARBLE
Minfong Ho

1. What family member of Dara's is killed?
   A. mother
   B. brother
   C. father

2. Who does Nea want to marry?
   A. Sarun
   B. Chnay
   C. Mr. Kem

3. What are Jantu and Dara doing when they get separated from their families?
   A. looking in the food truck
   B. playing with a toy village
   C. visiting another family

4. Who does not want to return home to plant rice?
   A. Jantu
   B. Sarun
   C. Mr. Kem

5. What do Nea and Dara do that women aren't supposed to do?
   A. march with the soldiers
   B. shoot a gun
   C. load rice sacks

6. What animal does Dara find in the kitchen?
   A. lizard
   B. monkey
   C. dog

7. Where do Dara and Nea find Jantu and Baby in Khao I Dang?
   A. officer's kitchen
   B. prison
   C. surgical ward

8. Who is killed by friendly gun fire?
   A. Nea
   B. Jantu
   C. Sarun

9. What ceremony is Sarun in at Nong Chan?
   A. flag raising ceremony
   B. medal ceremony
   C. enlistment ceremony

10. What does Chnay make for Dara?
    A. cow bell
    B. corn husk doll
    C. clay marble

THE COACH THAT NEVER CAME
Patricia Beatty

1. What present did Paul's grandmother give to him?
   A. Indian headband
   B. beaded belt
   C. belt buckle

2. Where does Paul find information about Billy Smart?
   A. in an old trunk
   B. in a museum
   C. from his son

3. What kind of contest does Paul enter?
   A. reading and essay
   B. swimming
   C. cereal box contest

4. What kind of Indian is Jay?
   A. Cherokee
   B. Ute
   C. Sioux

5. What is Kid Ruby's real name?
   A. Jesse Smart
   B. Joe Hartford
   C. Frank Hart

6. What was stolen from Paul's room?
   A. watch and ring
   B. buckle and letter
   C. wallet

7. What was found in the cave besides the gold and stagecoach?
   A. underground spring
   B. dead Indians
   C. Indian cave paintings

8. Who tied up Paul, Jay and Grandma?
   A. Matthew Smart
   B. Pete Dobbs
   C. Mr. Morse

9. Who was Billy Smart?
   A. rodeo rider
   B. U.S. marshal
   C. doctor

10. Where does Paul spend the summer?
    A. Colorado
    B. Delaware
    C. Wyoming

COLLIDESCOPE
Grace Chetwin

1. What two things does HAHN give Sky-Fire-Trail to wear?
   A. hat and gloves
   B. shoes and walkman
   C. silver blanket and headband

2. What is the LSRM?
   A. a repair unit
   B. a local radio station
   C. a coded message

3. What does HAHN not have?
   A. a heart
   B. a memory
   C. a ship

4. What does the Indian steal?
   A. food
   B. crystal time stone
   C. alien space ship

5. Why does HAHN think he is degenerating?
   A. he keeps forgetting things
   B. he is losing his coordination
   C. he is feeling emotions

6. Why does Sky-Fire-Trail dive into the river?
   A. to escape from his enemies
   B. to bring up mud from the bottom
   C. to get some fish

7. What does Frankie's mother do that bothers Frankie?
   A. she keeps her bedroom door locked
   B. she starts dressing strangely
   C. she starts dating

8. What does Frankie teach Sky-Fire-Trail how to do?
   A. read
   B. karate
   C. dance

9. What does Sky-Fire-Trail teach Frankie how to do?
   A. fish with her hands
   B. start a fire with sticks
   C. follow tracks

10. How do the three escape UnHAHN?
    A. they exchange ships with him
    B. they lock him in his ship
    C. they send him to the beginning of time

COME A STRANGER
Cynthia Voigt

1. What is different about Mina's second summer at dance camp?
   A. she eats alone
   B. she has a special bathroom
   C. she has a single room

2. Who meets Mina at the train station when she comes home from camp?
   A. Tamar Shipp
   B. her mother
   C. Zandor

3. What happened to Miss LaValle?
   A. she attempted suicide
   B. she was mugged
   C. she eloped

4. Who is Mina in love with?
   A. Samuel
   B. Tamar
   C. Louis

5. What sport does Mina enroll in?
   A. swimming
   B. bowling
   C. tennis

6. Who is Samuel named after?
   A. an actor
   B. Bullet
   C. his father's teacher

7. How was Bullet killed?
   A. car wreck
   B. small pox
   C. war

8. What do Mina's parents call her?
   A. Precious
   B. Trouble
   C. Sunshine

9. Why is Zandor kicked out of college?
   A. he was caught with marijuana
   B. he cheated on a test
   C. he flunked out

10. What good news does Alice tell Mina over the phone?
    A. she passed the GED
    B. she got a job
    C. she is pregnant

THE COOK CAMP
Gary Paulsen

1. What does the boy's grandmother call him?
    A. my little munchkin
    B. my little dumpling
    C. my little thimble

2. What eats out of the boy's hand?
    A. chipmunk
    B. rabbit
    C. raccoon

3. What does the boy ask his grandmother to teach him how to do?
    A. sew
    B. cook
    C. drive

4. What do the men do each day after lunch?
    A. go to work
    B. play cards
    C. sleep

5. What does Carl give to the boy?
    A. a puppy
    B. a hard hat
    C. a pocket knife

6. Where do Carl, the boy and his grandmother go every Friday?
    A. to hire more men
    B. to buy groceries
    C. to the movies

7. What does the boy's grandmother buy for him?
    A. candy
    B. toy truck
    C. cap and overalls

8. Why does the boy stay in the men's trailer?
    A. there isn't room in his grandmother's trailer
    B. grandmother's gone with an injured man
    C. the boy wants to sleep over with the men

9. Why does the boy cry in Gustaf's arms?
    A. he misses his mother
    B. his dog died
    C. he fell and hurt himself

10. Why does the grandmother swat flies all the time?
    A. she is angry with the boy's mother
    B. she doesn't like flies
    C. to feed them to the turtle

COVERUP
Jay Bennett

1. Where are Brad's parents?
   A. Hawaii
   B. cruise ship
   C. nursing home

2. Why is Ellen searching for her father?
   A. to tell him his wife is dead
   B. he sent her a letter
   C. to have him arrested

3. Where is Ellen from?
   A. Chicago
   B. California
   C. New York

4. Where is Ellen's father killed?
   A. at the beach
   B. on a back road
   C. in a warehouse

5. What does Alden claim he and Brad did on the way home from the party?
   A. stop at a bar
   B. pick up some girls
   C. swim in the ocean

6. Who calls Brad in the middle of the night?
   A. Alden
   B. Alden's father
   C. Alden's mother

7. What does Brad find in the road?
   A. watch
   B. medical alert bracelet
   C. purple heart medal

8. What does Alden do when Brad accuses him of killing someone?
   A. laugh it off
   B. prove him wrong
   C. try to run him down

9. Who filed a police report?
   A. Brad
   B. Alden
   C. Ellen

10. How long was Alden's prison sentence?
    A. 1 year
    B. 2 years
    C. 3 years

THE CROSSING
Gary Paulsen

1. What food does Manny ask Maria to give him for his trip across the bridge?
   A. tacos
   B. rice and beans
   C. chicken

2. What animal does one of the dancers have on stage at the bar?
   A. snake
   B. orangatang
   C. parrot

3. Why does Manny stand under the bridge?
   A. to catch coins
   B. to eat his lunch
   C. to bathe

4. What was Sergeant Locke doing when Manny tried to steal his wallet?
   A. peeing
   B. throwing up
   C. sleeping

5. What color is Manny's hair?
   A. blond
   B. black
   C. red

6. What does the way Manny eats remind Robert of?
   A. a starved dog
   B. a starved monkey
   C. a starved mouse

7. What does Robert buy two tickets for?
   A. carnival
   B. movie
   C. bull fight

8. What does Manny give to Robert?
   A. his sombrero
   B. a poster
   C. a map

9. How much money does the sergeant give Manny the first time?
   A. one dollar
   B. five dollars
   C. ten dollars

10. How is the sergeant killed?
    A. stabbed
    B. shot
    C. drowned

THE CRY OF THE CROW
Jean Craighead George

1. What do Mandy's brothers do when they need money for car parts?
   A. do lawn care
   B. pick fruit
   C. publish a local paper

2. What will Mandy not let Nina Terrance do?
   A. feed herself
   B. go into town
   C. be outside without a leash

3. Who does Nina harass?
   A. Barney
   B. Mandy
   C. Carver

4. Where does Mandy's father want to take the family?
   A. to the museum
   B. to New York City
   C. to the zoo

5. Who does Mandy confide in about Nina?
   A. Drummer
   B. Jack
   C. her mother

6. What does Nina do inside Mandy's house?
   A. open a window
   B. open the frig door
   C. open the front door

7. How does Mandy's father find out about the crow?
   A. Mandy told him
   B. from the newspaper
   C. eye witness news

8. What does Mandy's father want Mandy to do with the crow?
   A. kill it
   B. keep it
   C. set it free

9. Who shot Nina Terrance's family?
   A. Drummer
   B. Carver
   C. Jack

10. Who kills Nina?
    A. Mandy
    B. Mandy's father
    C. Drummer

CRYSTAL

Walter Dean Myers

1. Who is Crystal's best friend
   A. Pat
   B. Sister Gibb
   C. Loretta

2. What magazine does Crystal's agent want her to get in?
   A. Ebony
   B. La Femme
   C. Esquire

3. Where does Sister Gibb find the kitten she gave to Crystal?
   A. in a cage with a snake
   B. up a tree
   C. in the trash in a gunny sack

4. What did Crystal's father dream about being as a child?
   A. astronaut
   B. cowboy
   C. fireman

5. Who is not a model?
   A. Rowena
   B. Alyce
   C. Loretta

6. What does Crystal's mother do when Crystal says she wants to quit modeling?
   A. hit Crystal
   B. say she was thankful Crystal was finished
   C. break glasses

7. Why is Rowenna in the hospital?
   A. she tried to kill herself
   B. she overdosed on drugs
   C. she has anorexia

8. Who does Crystal call for help when she is at Joe Sydney's house?
   A. Loretta
   B. Rowena
   C. Sister Gibb

9. What does Crystal tell Joe Sidney at his house?
   A. she'll do anything to get the part
   B. she's not going to make the movie
   C. she's giving up modeling

10. What does Crystal ask Jerry for?
    A. pictures of Rowena
    B. a date
    C. a percentage of the profits

CURTAINS
R.L. Stine

1. Why does Rena wear Julie's clothes?
   A. her's are stolen
   B. her's are dirty
   C. her's are cut up

2. What does Rena find in her bunk bed?
   A. dead swan
   B. Hedy
   C. rattle snake

3. Who does Rena think she may have shot?
   A. Kenny
   B. Hedy
   C. Baxter

4. Who does Rena accidentally stab?
   A. Marcia
   B. Chip
   C. George

5. Who is jealous because all the boys like Rena?
   A. Hedy
   B. Marcia
   C. Julie

6. What does Rena think Baxter thrives on?
   A. danger
   B. cruelty
   C. applause

7. What does Baxter do that shocks everyone?
   A. he throws a temper tantrum
   B. he quits and goes home
   C. he pretends to hang himself

8. What does Baxter say acting is all about?
   A. contacts
   B. fear
   C. determination

9. Who's life does Rena save from drowning?
   A. George
   B. Cliff
   C. Julie

10. Who tries to kill Rena?
    A. George
    B. Hedy
    C. Baxter

DAGMAR SCHULTZ AND THE GREEN-EYED MONSTER
Lynn Hall

1. Who does Dagmar like?
   A. Eric
   B. Matthew
   C. Aron

2. What were Dagmar, Shelly and Ashley going to buy at the mall?
   A. dresses
   B. earrings
   C. present

3. What committee are Aron and Ashley on?
   A. decorating
   B. refreshments
   C. clean up

4. What terrible thing did Dagmar do to Ashley at the dance?
   A. spill punch on her dress
   B. pull down her dress
   C. trip her

5. How does Ashley react to being embarrassed at the dance?
   A. she cries
   B. she leaves
   C. she continues dancing

6. Who does Dagmar confide in about her plan to hurt herself?
   A. Ashley
   B. Neese
   C. Matthew

7. How does Dagmar decide to hurt herself?
   A. slit her wrists
   B. take some pills
   C. jump off a bridge

8. How has Dagmar's father always cheered her up in the past?
   A. by making funny faces
   B. by taking out his false teeth
   C. by telling her jokes

9. Who shows up to save Dagmar from hurting herself?
   A. everyone
   B. her parents
   C. the police

10. After Dagmar is saved what does everyone do for fun?
    A. jump into a snow bank
    B. drink hot chocolate
    C. tell stories

DANGER IN QUICKSAND SWAMP
Bill Wallace

1. What did the boys eat while on the island?
   A. coconuts
   B. fish
   C. alligator

2. What did Jake find in the dry river bed?
   A. a rowboat
   B. hidden treasure
   C. a skeleton

3. What was in the mason jar?
   A. treasure map
   B. old coins
   C. honey

4. What happened to Robert four years earlier?
   A. he went insane
   B. he was murdered
   C. he left home

5. What did Ben's sister, Lisa, find?
   A. her lost dog
   B. her father's gun
   C. the boy's secret hiding place

6. When the boys are stranded where do they spend the night?
   A. a cave
   B. a tree
   C. a shelter

7. Why did Kenny Grissom want to kill his brother, Theodore?
   A. to be an only child
   B. to marry Theodore's wife
   C. to live in the big house and own the bank

8. What did Kenny give his brother for Christmas every year?
   A. a stetson hat
   B. alligator boots
   C. leather gloves

9. How did the boys hide from the man who was after them?
   A. by covering themselves with mud
   B. by staying in the water
   C. by hiding in the rowboat

10. What was Ben's father hauling in the back of his logging truck?
    A. alligators
    B. logs
    C. snakes

THE DEAD MAN IN INDIAN CREEK
Mary Downing Hahn

1. What does Parker's mother repair?
    A. dolls
    B. clothes
    C. furniture

2. What does Parker always get teased about?
    A. being smart
    B. being fat
    C. being cute

3. What does Matt do at the police station?
    A. throw up
    B. spill his coke
    C. stutter

4. How was the dead man in Indian Creek killed?
    A. knifed
    B. shot
    C. drown

5. What do Matt and Parker build at the quarry?
    A. snow castle
    B. tree house
    C. fort

6. What does Evans hide inside the dolls' heads?
    A. diamonds
    B. microfilm
    C. drugs

7. Where do Matt and Parker hide while Evans is looking for them?
    A. Jennifer's basement
    B. Flynn's van
    C. Pam's house

8. How does the evidence arrive at the police station?
    A. in a baby carriage
    B. on a tricycle
    C. in a jack-o-lantern

9. How is Flynn captured?
    A. he falls into the quarry
    B. he is trapped in a pit
    C. he is hit with a club

10. Why is Pam in surgery?
    A. gun shot wound
    B. broken leg
    C. broken jaw

DEALING WITH DRAGONS
Patricia C. Wrede

1. How does Alianora get rid of the wizards?
   A. she casts a spell
   B. she kills them with rocks
   C. she melts them with water

2. What happens to the prince who tries to steal the magic water?
   A. turns to stone
   B. captured
   C. poisoned

3. Why does Cimorene cast a magic spell?
   A. to become fireproof
   B. to cure warts
   C. to call up wizards

4. What do Cimorene's three magic feathers do?
   A. protect her
   B. take her anywhere
   C. make her invisible

5. What happens to the king of the dragons?
   A. he gets a queen
   B. he is taken on a journey
   C. he is poisoned

6. What must you do to become king of the dragons?
   A. own a princess
   B. carry a special stone
   C. kill a knight

7. What are dragons allergic to?
   A. dwarves
   B. red mushrooms
   C. wizard's staff

8. What is constantly bothering Cimorene?
   A. dragonflies
   B. knights rescuing her
   C. dragon's breath

9. What do the wizards steal?
   A. book
   B. Cimorene
   C. dragon

10. What happened to the dragon, Woraug?
    A. he became a toad
    B. he became king
    C. he was slain

DEAR MOM, GET ME OUT OF HERE!

Ellen Conford

1. What does Barbara do after lunch each day?
   A. ride her horse
   B. have her voice lesson
   C. watch her favorite soap

2. What is Wendell Warren's pet?
   A. rat
   B. rooster
   C. pig

3. What does Wendell Warren teach the other boys how to do?
   A. dance
   B. pick locks
   C. flirt

4. What does Sergio have in his room?
   A. machine gun
   B. sewing machine
   C. teddy bear

5. What do Paul and Chris look for when they break into Pickle's house?
   A. food
   B. map
   C. book

6. What does Sergio lead?
   A. a revolt
   B. a boys' choir
   C. a search party

7. What do Chris and Paul think Pickle's crime is?
   A. murdering his family with an axe
   B. burning down the Presbyterian church
   C. robbing the Denver mint

8. What do the boys do to help capture Pickles?
   A. they hold him at gun point and wait for the police
   B. they get him to try to kill them
   C. recreate the crime on stage

9. Who turns out to be the real criminal?
   A. Pickles
   B. Bucky
   C. Sergio

10. Who agrees to invest money to save the school?
    A. Chris's father
    B. Uncle Jack
    C. Barbara

DEATH WALK

Walt Morey

1. How does Joel sprain his ankle?
   A. going over a waterfall
   B. plane crash
   C. snowmobile crash

2. What does Joel's father do?
   A. criminal lawyer
   B. judge
   C. policeman

3. Who tries to kill Joel?
   A. Emmitt and Hank
   B. Hank and Blackie
   C. Blackie and Fawn

4. Who gets shot?
   A. Blackie
   B. Fawn
   C. Joel

5. Why does Joel not want to face his father?
   A. he broke up with his girl
   B. he was suspended
   C. he lost a fight

6. Who burns down Hank's cabin?
   A. Mike
   B. Joel
   C. Emmitt

7. How does Mike get hurt?
   A. he fell on the ice
   B. he stepped in a trap
   C. a boulder rolled over him

8. How does Hank die?
   A. he sank in quicksand
   B. ice block fell on him
   C. he froze to death

9. How does Emmitt die?
   A. he was attacked by a bear
   B. he was buried in an avalanche
   C. he was speared

10. Who brings Joel back to civilization?
    A. photographers
    B. trappers
    C. his father

DECEMBER STILLNESS
Mary Downing Hahn

1. Where does Kelly buy her clothes?
   A. at the mall
   B. at K-mart
   C. at the thrift shop

2. Where do Kelly and her friends go every Thursday night?
   A. to the library
   B. to play tennis
   C. shopping

3. Why does Kelly talk to the bag man the first time?
   A. for a joke
   B. out of curiosity
   C. she wants to help

4. What do Kelly and the bag man do together?
   A. read the newspaper
   B. feed the ducks
   C. go for a walk

5. What does the bag man do with the sandwiches Kelly makes for him?
   A. he eats them
   B. he saves them
   C. he throws them away

6. What does the bag man hit Kelly with?
   A. his fist
   B. a magazine
   C. a chair

7. What kind of books does the bag man read at the library?
   A. mysteries
   B. romance novels
   C. war books

8. What does Kelly do with the picture she drew of the bag man?
   A. hang it on her wall
   B. leave it at the Vietnam memorial
   C. give it to the bag man

9. How does the bag man die?
   A. hit by a car
   B. cancer
   C. old age

10. What does Kelly's father do?
    A. he is a corporate attorney
    B. he is a preacher
    C. he is a golf pro

DEENIE
Judy Bloom

1. Where does Deenie's dad work?
   A. at a retail store
   B. at a gas station
   C. at a butcher shop

2. What does Janet carry for good luck?
   A. chicken's foot
   B. rabbit's foot
   C. four leaf clover

3. Who tells Deenie's parents there could be something wrong with her back?
   A. the gym teacher
   B. the modeling agency
   C. the school nurse

4. What did Deenie do to show her anger at having to wear the brace?
   A. tear up her room
   B. cut her hair off
   C. refuse to wear it

5. What does the principal want Deenie to do?
   A. go to special classes
   B. not take gym class
   C. ride the handicapped bus

6. When can Deenie take off her brace?
   A. to sleep
   B. to swim
   C. to dance

7. What can Deenie not do with her brace?
   A. dance
   B. sleep
   C. see her food

8. What happens when Deenie refuses to wear an undershirt?
   A. she gets sores
   B. she gets a rash
   C. she gets bruises

9. What does the brace do?
   A. rip her clothes
   B. cause her to lose her friends
   C. cause her to be made fun of

10. What do Midge and Janet buy for Deenie?
    A. a nightgown
    B. flowers
    C. candy

DEVIL'S RACE
Avi

1. What does Ann like to do?
   A. fish
   B. hunt
   C. backpack

2. What is "Devil's Race"?
   A. creek
   B. trail
   C. mountain

3. What does John Pride leave at the cemetery?
   A. canteen
   B. flowers
   C. cross

4. Who dies of exhaustion?
   A. Uncle Tom
   B. Uncle Dave
   C. Aunt Nora

5. Who does the ancestor, John Proud, try to use but is unable to?
   A. John Proud
   B. Uncle Dave
   C. Ann

6. How does the ancestor, John Proud, get rid of Ann's parents temporarily?
   A. school meeting
   B. car accident
   C. fire

7. What does the ancestor get John Proud to follow him into?
   A. lion's den
   B. Hell
   C. gunnery range

8. What is Ann doing when she almost falls off the mountain?
   A. following a butterfly
   B. brushing off an ant
   C. running from a bear

9. What does Ann hurt?
   A. her ankle
   B. her collarbone
   C. her head

10. How does John Proud defeat his ancestor?
    A. by embracing him
    B. by driving a stake through his heart
    C. by praying

DINKY HOCKER SHOOTS SMACK
M.E. Kerr

1. What does Tucker want to be when he grows up?
   A. grocery store manager
   B. court clerk
   C. librarian

2. What does Tucker's father say his new business will be?
   A. health foods
   B. sports gym
   C. bicycle shop

3. What does Natalia do when she's nervous?
   A. rhyme
   B. bite her nails
   C. stutter

4. Who does Tucker get to take Dinky to the dance?
   A. Nader
   B. P. John
   C. Marcus

5. What is wrong with P. John?
   A. addict
   B. mentally slow
   C. fat

6. What is Dinky's real name?
   A. Dinks
   B. Susan
   C. Diana

7. What does Tucker give Natalia for Christmas?
   A. stationary
   B. plant
   C. balloons

8. What is Tucker's mother's big news?
   A. she's going to have a baby
   B. she's going to law school
   C. she's going to quit her job

9. Why is Tucker's father upset with Jingle?
   A. he burned down their store
   B. he wants to move in with them
   C. he wants to take over the store

10. How does Dinky feel when she sees P. John after he returns from his aunt's?
    A. embarrassed
    B. excited
    C. scared

DIXIE STORMS
Barbara Hall

1. What does Bodean always say?
   A. Do me a favor, Make me an offer
   B. Give me a break, Get off my back
   C. Make my day, Are you for real?

2. What do Flood and Dutch's father argue about?
   A. child rearing
   B. John Deere tractors
   C. women

3. What crop do the Peytons grow?
   A. tobacco
   B. wheat
   C. cotton

4. What does Dutch find under Flood's mattress?
   A. money
   B. letters
   C. journal

5. Why is the family mad at Uncle Eugene?
   A. he dropped out of school
   B. he married an outsider
   C. he left the farm

6. What does Flood forbid Bodean and Dutch to do?
   A. ride on the tracker
   B. change the light bulbs
   C. get the mail

7. What does Dutch tell Norma in order to hurt her?
   A. her parents are getting a divorce
   B. she can't wait until Norma goes home
   C. everyone is talking behind her back

8. Who leaves the farm besides Norma?
   A. Dutch
   B. Flood
   C. Bodean

9. Who gives Dutch's dad money to save the tractor?
   A. Aunt Mary
   B. Flood
   C. Uncle Eugene

10. Who does Flood start dating?
    A. Norma
    B. Lucy
    C. Becky

THE DOLL IN THE GARDEN
Mary Downing Hahn

1. What is the name of the white cat?
    A. Furball
    B. Fluffy
    C. Snowball

2. What is wrong with Louisa?
    A. consumption
    B. small pox
    C. whooping cough

3. What do Louisa and Ashley have in common?
    A. their fathers' are dead
    B. they are both eight
    C. they both like to play with dolls

4. Who returns the doll to Louisa?
    A. Kristi
    B. Miss Cooper
    C. Ashley

5. Who does Louisa live with?
    A. her grandparents
    B. her spinster sister
    C. her aunt

6. What was the doll's name?
    A. Mary Beth
    B. Anna Maria
    C. Sarah Jane

7. Where is Kristi's special place?
    A. by the pond
    B. in the meadow
    C. in a tree house

8. What does the note in the box say?
    A. Rest in peace
    B. Please forgive me, I am sorry.
    C. To whoever finds this doll please take good care of her

9. What kind of headstone does Louisa have?
    A. pink angel
    B. flat brass plaque
    C. granite cross

10. Who is Max?
    A. Miss Cooper's dog
    B. Miss Cooper's son
    C. Kristi's cat

DON'T CARE HIGH
Gordon Korman

1. What is unusual about Mike Otis' clothing?
   A. safety pins in the pants
   B. chains for a belt
   C. red scarves around each knee

2. What does Mike's car look like?
   A. a hearse
   B. a German staff car
   C. a gangster's car

3. What does Sheldon take from the school office?
   A. Mike's school records
   B. the public announcement system
   C. disciplinary notices

4. How do Sheldon and Paul distribute the Otis Report?
   A. through homeroom teachers
   B. in the halls on roller skates
   C. put stacks in restrooms at night

5. What nickname does Sheldon give to Paul?
   A. Cop out
   B. Enthusiasm
   C. Ambition

6. What does Paul take a picture of for his photography class?
   A. a junk yard
   B. a smashed banana
   C. Mike's car

7. What is Mike's physics project?
   A. sewer system
   B. air pollution
   C. recycling

8. What unites the students?
   A. school dance
   B. the trashing of their school
   C. Mike being kicked out of office

9. What does Fieldstein control?
   A. the restrooms
   B. the lockers
   C. the cafeteria

10. What does Mr. Morrison do at the Laguna game?
    A. lead a cheer
    B. get kicked out of the game
    C. coach the team

DON'T LOOK BEHIND YOU
Lois Duncan

1. Where does April's family move to?
   A. Florida
   B. California
   C. New York

2. Where does April's old tennis partner, Jo Simmons, recognize her at?
   A. Smokey Mountain National Park
   B. Disney World
   C. Fort Lauderdale Beach

3. What does April's mother have to give up?
   A. publishing her books
   B. smoking
   C. teaching aerobics

4. What does April miss when they move?
   A. the senior trip
   B. the prom
   C. the domino tournament

5. When April runs away who does she expect to live with?
   A. Jo Simmons
   B. her grandmother, Loelei
   C. Jim Peterson

6. What happens to April's grandmother?
   A. she is robbed
   B. she is run off the road
   C. her arm is broken

7. Who killed Jim Peterson at the hotel?
   A. a man dressed as a maid
   B. a man dressed as a waiter
   C. a man dressed as a bellhop

8. What does Mike Vamp keep stealing from Lorelei and April?
   A. car keys
   B. road maps
   C. women's clothes

9. How does April escape from her house?
   A. by crawling down the hall
   B. by going through a trap door in the attic
   C. by climbing through the window

10. What does April kill Mike Vamp with?
    A. tire iron
    B. tennis racket
    C. baseball bat

DON'T RENT MY ROOM
Judi Angell

1. Why does Nathan want to quit school and do for a year?
   A. commercial fishing
   B. go to Europe
   C. go backpacking

2. What does Chip look for when he takes people out in a boat?
   A. oil spills
   B. whales
   C. icebergs

3. What is on the screened in porch?
   A. a ghost
   B. ping pong table
   C. an alligator

4. What does Lucy want to work on?
   A. an airplane engine
   B. an environmental project
   C. her homework

5. Who does Lucy want to live with in New York City?
   A. her girlfriend
   B. her father
   C. her grandmother

6. Why did Mercer Scottwood hate his grandson, Howard?
   A. Howard killed him
   B. Howard wrecked his car
   C. Howard stole the family jewels

7. What does Joan know how to fix?
   A. a hole in the roof
   B. her car
   C. breakfast

8. What do all the guests in the inn help do?
   A. put up posters
   B. put up decorations
   C. close the shutters on the windows

9. What is wrong in the basement?
   A. smells like a skunk
   B. flooded
   C. a wall caved in

10. What do the Webers have a hard time finding?
    A. the keys to their car
    B. a permanent waitress
    C. the family pet

DOWN RIVER
Will Hobbs

1. What do the kids call the program they are in?
   A. Hikers in Hell
   B. Thugs not Drugs
   C. Hoods in the Woods

2. Who didn't float the Colorado River?
   A. Heather
   B. Pug
   C. Rita

3. Who can't read?
   A. Freddy
   B. Troy
   C. Adam

4. What does Star always have with her?
   A. diary
   B. tarot cards
   C. Bible

5. What does Troy throw in the river that shocks everyone?
   A. his credit cards
   B. his life preserver
   C. the river guide

6. What do Troy and Pug put in Freddie's sleeping bag?
   A. snake
   B. scorpion
   C. yellow jacket

7. Who does Star live with after the rafting trip is over?
   A. Rita
   B. Freddy
   C. Jessie

8. What kind of job does Adam get?
   A. grooming dogs
   B. junior counselor for Al
   C. cook for a day care center

9. What does Adam pretend he is?
   A. ninja
   B. superman
   C. rock star

10. What is Freddy's rehabilitation job?
    A. putting out forest fires
    B. building a road
    C. cleaning trash off the highway

DR. DREDD'S WAGON OF WONDERS
Bill Brittain

1. What does Dr. Dredd agree to do for the village?
    A. provide rain
    B. provide medicine
    C. make the cows give milk

2. Who does Ellen find in the wood shed?
    A. Antaeus
    B. Bufu
    C. baby dragon

3. How does Dr. Dredd find Bufu?
    A. he follows the smell of rain
    B. he follows his footprints
    C. he reads tea leaves

4. What does Dr. Dredd use the whip on at Ellen's house?
    A. the chickens
    B. a pillow
    C. Ellen's mother

5. Where does Antaeus get his strength?
    A. from Dr. Dredd
    B. from the sun
    C. from the ground

6. Who fights Antaeus to save Calvin?
    A. Sumner Beezum
    B. Packer Vickery
    C. Sven Hensen

7. What does Magda give Ellen?
    A. a wooden staff
    B. a magic potion
    C. a cat

8. What do Calvin and Ellen do to the black knight?
    A. push him into a well
    B. run him through with a sword
    C. trap him in a net

9. What is Dr. Dredd afraid of?
    A. cemeteries
    B. churches
    C. Magda

10. How is the dragon killed?
    A. sword
    B. lightening
    C. avalanche

THE DRAGON AND THE THIEF
Gillian Bradshaw

1. What killed Prahotep's father?
    A. crocodile
    B. snake
    C. shark

2. Why does Prahotep have to leave the rock quarry?
    A. he was caught stealing some water
    B. he dropped a hammer on Kenna's arm
    C. he killed a prisoner

3. What does Prahotep buy for Hathor?
    A. boat
    B. princess
    C. pair of glasses

4. How does Nefersenet find Prahotep?
    A. through spies
    B. through a magic bracelet
    C. through a crystal ball

5. How does Hathor help Prahotep and Baki escape from Nefersenet's men?
    A. she drops boulders on his men
    B. she breathes fire down on his men
    C. she drops wet linen on his men

6. What is Prahotep's cloak made out of?
    A. gazelle skin
    B. sheep skin
    C. lion skin

7. How do Prahotep and Baki escape from the city of Elephantine?
    A. through a storm drain
    B. they dress as priests and leave through the gate
    C. over the wall in a basket

8. What do Prahotep and Baki disguise themselves as to fool Nefersenet?
    A. soldiers
    B. fishermen
    C. date farmers

9. What does Hathor promise to give Prahotep for helping her get to Nubia?
    A. a job
    B. nothing
    C. gold necklace

10. What enchanted animal carries Prahotep to Nefersenet?
    A. unicorn
    B. falcon
    C. winged monkey

THE DRAGON OF MIDDLETHORPE
Anne Leo Ellis

1. Who lives alone in the forest?
   A. Mad Rose
   B. the dragon
   C. Fife

2. Why are the townspeople afraid of Rose?
   A. she is cross-eyed
   B. they believe she put a curse on a hunting party
   C. they believe she is a witch

3. What does Rose believe about dragons?
   A. they do not exist
   B. they are harmless
   C. they have magical powers

4. Who gets beat up in the apothecary shop?
   A. Mad Rose
   B. Master Clement
   C. Kate's father

5. How do Fife and his mule die?
   A. fell on his sword
   B. burned by the dragon
   C. drown in a bog

6. What does Kate throw at the dragon?
   A. magic rope
   B. dirt and rocks
   C. powdered unicorn horn

7. Who does Kate like?
   A. Tim
   B. Fife
   C. Master Clement

8. What kind of apprenticeship is Tim in?
   A. apothecary
   B. metal worker
   C. glassmaker

9. What does Kate see the morning after the battle?
   A. apothecary's silver box
   B. white unicorn
   C. dragon

10. What does Kate's father agree to let her do?
    A. become a soldier
    B. be apprenticed to the apothecary
    C. get married

THE DRAGON'S BOY

Jane Yolen

1. When do the other boys accept Artos?
   A. when he kills his first dragon
   B. when he bests them in a duel
   C. when he gets his sword

2. What does the dragon teach Artos to play?
   A. three cup game
   B. riddle game
   C. poker

3. What is in the pouch Artos wears around his neck?
   A. gold ring
   B. map
   C. magic whistle

4. What does Artos name his sword?
   A. Blessed One
   B. Inter Linea
   C. Dark Slayer

5. What does the dragon ask Artos to bring him?
   A. a princess
   B. a riddle he hasn't heard
   C. stew with meat

6. What does Mag ask for in return for giving Artos food?
   A. coins
   B. a kiss
   C. an audience with the king

7. How does Artos pay for his sword?
   A. gold coins
   B. with work
   C. red stone

8. What does the dragon call Artos?
   A. Son of Kingdoms
   B. Son of Pentedragon
   C. Son of Mountain

9. Who is the dragon?
   A. Old Linn
   B. the king
   C. his mother

10. Who stole Artos from his mother?
    A. Old Linn
    B. the king
    C. the dragon

ENCORE
Joan Lowery Nixon

1. Who does Erin like?
   A. Eddie
   B. Jake
   C. Bobby

2. Where is Erin when she learns her show has been cancelled?
   A. at home
   B. at a cast party
   C. at her agent's office

3. Why does Erin think Cassie is a bad mother?
   A. she is never home
   B. she never lets her do anything
   C. she makes her wear old fashioned clothes

4. Why do Erin's parents stare at her when Eddie brings her home from dinner?
   A. she has a black eye
   B. her sleeve is ripped
   C. her hair is purple

5. Why is Erin's show cancelled?
   A. no backers
   B. bad ratings
   C. two actors quit

6. What kind of movie is Abby making?
   A. comedy
   B. mystery
   C. drama

7. What does Eddie want to buy?
   A. a Bronco
   B. a Harley
   C. jeep

8. Where does Erin take Tina?
   A. mall
   B. movie
   C. zoo

9. Who directs Abby's movie?
   A. Abby
   B. Erin's father
   C. Bobby

10. Where is a scene from Abby's movie shown?
    A. on TV as a commercial
    B. at a banquet honoring Abby
    C. at a theater as a preview

THE FACE ON THE MILK CARTON
Caroline B. Cooney

1. What does Janie ask her parents for?
   A. her birth certificate
   B. her grandmother's earrings
   C. permission to have a party

2. Who is Janie's best friend?
   A. Lizzie
   B. Reeves
   C. Caroline

3. Where does Janie get her first kiss?
   A. in a pile of leaves
   B. at the school dance
   C. on her front porch

4. What does Janie find in the attic?
   A. her birth certificate
   B. the dress she was taken in
   C. her baby pictures

5. Where was Janie taken from?
   A. her backyard
   B. school
   C. a shopping mall

6. Who stole Janie?
   A. her neighbor
   B. a doctor
   C. her parents' daughter

7. Who do the parents who raised Janie think she is?
   A. their granddaughter
   B. their daughter
   C. a stolen child

8. What is Janie allergic to?
   A. cats
   B. penicillin
   C. milk products

9. Who does Reeves tell about Janie?
   A. his teacher
   B. his sister
   C. the police

10. What has Janie always wanted to change about herself?
    A. her nose
    B. her name
    C. her personality

A FAMILY APART

Joan Lowery Nixon

1. What did Mike do that caused him to be sent on the orphan train?
    A. steal food
    B. stab a man
    C. picked pockets

2. What did Frances and her mother do for a living?
    A. scrub floors
    B. beg in the streets
    C. take care of children

3. What was Frances required to do on the train because she was dressed as a boy?
    A. put out a brush fire
    B. defend a woman
    C. play with the boys

4. What mistake does Frances make at the party?
    A. she admires the lace on a lady's dress
    B. she picked up a cloth doll
    C. she says she can sew

5. Why does Frankie take the runaway slaves to the Muellers?
    A. no one would suspect a girl
    B. no one would suspect a child
    C. because Jake was too sick to do it

6. What does Frankie have a hard time understanding?
    A. why people want to help the slaves
    B. what sacrifice means
    C. what the underground railroad is

7. What did Frankie wrap the cheese in for the trip home?
    A. newspaper
    B. towel
    C. shawl

8. Who tells Frankie's new parents that she is a girl?
    A. Frances
    B. Katherine
    C. Petey

9. How come the Marshal decides not to take Frances into town for a trial?
    A. no evidence
    B. she is a child
    C. he thinks what she did was right

10. Who does Frances believe has been adopted by bad people?
    A. Mike
    B. Megan
    C. Peg

FAMILY REUNION
Caroline B. Cooney

1. Where does Shelley's mother live?
    A. Paris
    B. Cheyenne
    C. London

2. What does Angus sell?
    A. magazine subscriptions
    B. shares in a bomb shelter
    C. stock in a babysitting service

3. What does Angus carry around with him?
    A. fake leg
    B. microphone
    C. rubber snake

4. What word does everyone use to describe Shelley's family?
    A. emotional
    B. unstable
    C. serious

5. What does Shelley's family call the family hosting the reunion?
    A. The Snobs
    B. the Happys
    C. The Perfects

6. What does Shelley think the big secret is?
    A. Angus is adopted
    B. her father had a wife before Celeste
    C. her father has another son

7. What did Shelley's father do for Toby and his mother?
    A. support them while she went to school
    B. set them up in a business
    C. pay for Toby's father's funeral

8. Who does Shelley's father say he doesn't want to meet?
    A. Brett
    B. DeWitt
    C. Toby

9. Why is Aunt Maggie upset?
    A. her party bombed
    B. Brett ran away
    C. Toby didn't come to the party

10. What decision does Shelley make while at the reunion?
    A. to visit her mother
    B. to visit Chicago
    C. to date Toby

THE FANTASTIC FRESHMAN
Bill Brittain

1. What does Stanley do to Jerry the first day of school?
   A. give him a black eye
   B. stuff him in a locker
   C. choke him with his tie

2. What does the student council stick Stanley with all the work for?
   A. planning the dance
   B. planning the pep assembly
   C. planning the fundraiser

3. Who discovers Stanley is under a spell?
   A. Buster
   B. Peachy
   C. Stonewall

4. Who helps Stanley with the arrangements for the dance?
   A. Norma
   B. Buster
   C. Peachy

5. Who does Norma go to the dance with?
   A. Stanley
   B. Stonewall
   C. Ray

6. Why does Stanley run home from the pond?
   A. Jerry, the bully, is after him
   B. the green suit is after him
   C. he's late for a date with Peachy

7. Where does Stanley find the pyramid?
   A. in his sock drawer
   B. in his locker
   C. inside Dexter Dragon

8. What does Peachy Keene insist that Stanley do?
   A. stay away from her
   B. learn manners
   C. get her a date with Ray

9. Where does Stanley break his leg?
   A. school dance
   B. football game
   C. stairs at home

10. Where does Stanley put the glass pyramid to get rid of it?
    A. in the pond
    B. buried it in the backyard
    C. in the trash

FAST TALK ON A SLOW TRACK
Rita Williams-Garcia

1. What does Denzel sell?
   A. encyclopedias
   B. magazines
   C. candy and cookies

2. Why is Wendy angry with Denzel?
   A. he didn't take her to the prom
   B. he isn't going to her college
   C. he pretends he doesn't know her

3. What does Denzel's father refuse to do?
   A. go to church
   B. talk to white people
   C. carry a gun

4. What is Denzel's legal given name?
   A. Zello
   B. Dinizulu
   C. Dennis

5. What team is the worst at selling?
   A. Mello and Denzel
   B. Mikie
   C. Shawanda and Bad

6. Why does Denzel think Mello is going to kill himself?
   A. Mello keeps talking about suicide
   B. Mello is hanging from an overpass bridge
   C. Mello is depressed about his girl

7. Who does Mello want to marry?
   A. Shawanda
   B. Lydia
   C. Ymangila

8. Who beat up Denzel?
   A. Bad
   B. Mello
   C. Vernon

9. Who can't read?
   A. Mello
   B. Bad
   C. Shawanda

10. What does Denzel do at the end of the summer?
    A. go to Princeton
    B. go to a local college
    C. get a job

FATHOM FIVE
Robert Westall

1. Where does Cam live?
    A. on Low Street
    B. on a tugboat
    C. in the cemetery

2. What do Chas and Cem dig through the trash looking for?
    A. Gold Flake cigarette pack
    B. English battery
    C. bloody knife

3. What do Chas and Cem build?
    A. raft
    B. spy glass
    C. metal detector

4. What do Cem, Chas and Sheila ask the merchants of Low Street for?
    A. scrap metal
    B. hard cardboard
    C. information

5. What is Audrey?
    A. police dog
    B. German spy
    C. reporter

6. What do Sheila and Audrey dress as when they go out at night looking for the man who bought the watch?
    A. rich ladies
    B. whores
    C. waitresses

7. Who was kidnapped?
    A. Audrey
    B. Sheila
    C. Chas

8. Who was murdered?
    A. Dick Burley
    B. Nelly
    C. Robert McGill

9. Who was the spy?
    A. Sven
    B. Dick Burley
    C. Mr. Kallonas

10. How did the spy try to kill Chas?
    A. drown him in the tugboat
    B. knife him in a bar brawl
    C. smother him in Nelly's brothel

FELL
M.E.Kerr

1. What kind of camp is Ping going to?
   A. tennis
   B. acting
   C. magician

2. How much does Pengree pay Fell to switch places with his son?
   A. $20,000
   B. $50,000
   C. $100,000

3. What was Fell's dad's occupation?
   A. private detective
   B. tourist guide
   C. engineer

4. What does Fern paint?
   A. mountains
   B. oceans
   C. people

5. What is the name of the secret club at Gardner?
   A. The Fates
   B. The Elite
   C. The Sevens

6. What is the first thing new students at Gardner must do?
   A. climb the tower
   B. plant a tree
   C. say the Gardner pledge

7. Who is missing?
   A. Dib
   B. Lasher
   C. Mr. Pengree

8. What did Fell's dad give him?
   A. fishing rod
   B. gun
   C. large inheritance

9. What are Mr. and Mrs. Pengree really?
   A. spies
   B. jewel thieves
   C. drug smugglers

10. How does Ping's mother die?
    A. drowned
    B. electrocuted
    C. shot

FELL BACK
M.E. Kerr

1. What is unusual about Nina's looks?
   A. she has a dimple in her chin
   B. she has one blue eye and one green eye
   C. she has a dragonfly tattoo

2. What subject does Fell tutor Nina in?
   A. writing
   B. math
   C. science

3. What shocking news does Nina learn about Eddie while at Dragonland?
   A. he's married
   B. he's an alcoholic
   C. he's a cop

4. What does Nina's father hire Fell to do?
   A. spy on the Sevens
   B. be his informer
   C. date his daughter

5. Where does Fell hide to see who Creery meets at the house?
   A. in a phone booth
   B. in a closet
   C. in a box

6. Who does Creery meet at the apartment?
   A. David Deems
   B. Lauren Lasher
   C. Dibs

7. What is Meatloaf?
   A. horse
   B. raccoon
   C. dog

8. Who killed Cyril Creery?
   A. David Deems
   B. Lowell Hunter
   C. Eddie Dragon

9. What was Deems arrested for being involved in?
   A. illegal drugs
   B. smuggling
   C. stealing jewels

10. Who was Eddie Dragon?
    A. an FBI agent
    B. a high school dropout
    C. a rock star

FELL DOWN
M.E. Kerr

1. What do the ventriloquists call their dolls?
   A. dummies
   B. my block of wood
   C. figures

2. What is Plumsie worth?
   A. $25,000
   B. $14,000
   C. $3,000

3. Where did Lenny want Plum to go when he died?
   A. to the Vent Haven Museum
   B. to another vent
   C. to his sister

4. Who do Lenny and Nels like?
   A. Keats
   B. Laura
   C. Celeste

5. What does Nels call Lenny?
   A. Mr. Original
   B. Handy
   C. Tra La

6. Who does Nels want to kidnap?
   A. Annette
   B. Celeste
   C. Plumsie

7. What does Celeste always want?
   A. donuts
   B. peanuts
   C. snickers

8. Why did the cruise ship return two days early?
   A. they were hijacked
   B. President Kennedy was killed
   C. a passenger had a heart attack

9. Who disappeared and has never been found?
   A. Nels
   B. Lenny
   C. Fen

10. Who really is Plumsie?
    A. Celeste
    B. Annette
    C. Fen

THE FIGHTING GROUND
Avi

1. What language does the enemy speak?
    A. German
    B. English
    C. French

2. What does one of the enemy soldiers help Jonathan do?
    A. haul water
    B. dig a grave
    C. gather wood

3. Where do the enemy soldiers find Jonathan?
    A. in the woods
    B. behind the barn
    C. in a field

4. How many soldiers capture Jonathan?
    A. 1
    B. 3
    C. 10

5. What does Jonathan do while captive?
    A. start a fire
    B. feed the chickens
    C. milk a cow

6. Why are the man and woman killed?
    A. they are British
    B. they are American
    C. they are Tori traitors

7. How many soldiers does Jonathan kill?
    A. 0
    B. 3
    C. 5

8. What does Jonathan escape with?
    A. his gun
    B. a horse
    C. a child

9. Who does Jonathan try to save?
    A. the Captain
    B. his captors
    C. the man and woman

10. What does Jonathan do with the gun he borrowed?
    A. return it
    B. destroy it
    C. lose it

FINDERS KEEPERS
Emily Rodda

1. Where is the barrier weakest?
   A. near the large clocks
   B. near the airport
   C. near the stream

2. What happens when Patrick gets near what he is to find?
   A. a whistle goes off
   B. a pin beeps
   C. he gets chills

3. What is Lucky Lamont?
   A. robot
   B. computer
   C. man

4. How is Patrick told what to find?
   A. in morse code
   B. in riddles
   C. in charades

5. What does Patrick find for Clyde O'Brien?
   A. radio
   B. key
   C. book

6. What does O'Brien really want?
   A. his divorce decree
   B. a micro chip
   C. his grandfather's will

7. Who does Patrick accidentally bring back on his second trip?
   A. Estelle
   B. Clare
   C. Boopie

8. What happens when a person stays too long on the wrong side of the barrier?
   A. they can't return
   B. they forget the other side
   C. they fade out

9. How does Patrick return the pink bunny?
   A. he mails it
   B. he throws it from his kitchen
   C. he has Clare deliver it

10. What happens when Wendy Minelli gets the bunny back?
    A. she wins a prize
    B. she gets her job back
    C. the bunny comes alive

FINGERS

William Sleator

1. What does the old man Sam runs into after each concert mention to Sam?
   A. that he enjoyed the concert
   B. that Humphrey is a fake
   C. how Sam changed the music

2. How does Sam's mother make Humphrey believe he wrote the music?
   A. she drugs him
   B. she casts a spell on him
   C. she hypnotizes him

3. What is in the package Sam finds on the train?
   A. a book about Magyar
   B. a violin
   C. a severed head

4. What instrument is haunted in the story the gypsies tell?
   A. flute
   B. violin
   C. banjo

5. What is inside the handkerchief bundle on Humphrey's bed?
   A. a gypsy's crystal ball
   B. an old manuscript
   C. two hands

6. Who tells Humphrey the truth about who wrote the Magyar pieces?
   A. Bridgette
   B. Sam
   C. Luc

7. How does Sam get out of the locked hotel room?
   A. he threw tied bed sheets out the window
   B. he breaks the door down
   C. room service unlocked the door

8. Who is the old man in black?
   A. the ghost of Laszlo Magyar
   B. Laszlo Magyar's son
   C. a music critic

9. What does Bridgette do with Laszlo's manuscripts?
   A. burn them
   B. steal them
   C. sell them

10. Where do Sam, Humphrey and Laszlo run away to?
    A. an island
    B. the wilderness of Canada
    C. a castle in France

FIVE-FINGER DISCOUNT
Barthe De Clements

1. How does Edward find out about Jerry's dad?
   A. from his father
   B. from a newspaper
   C. from a letter

2. What does Jerry's mom do for a living?
   A. waitress
   B. sales clerk
   C. grocery cashier

3. What does Edward steal from Jerry and ruin?
   A. his jacket
   B. his homework
   C. his lunch

4. What is a swirly?
   A. a type of milk shake
   B. flushing the toilet with a head in it
   C. a game

5. Where does Jerry go to escape from Edward Troller?
   A. the nurse
   B. the counselor
   C. the library

6. Who saves Jerry when he is in the principal's office?
   A. his mother
   B. Grace's father
   C. Mr. Hillard

7. What does Jerry get with his five-finger discount?
   A. a baseball cap
   B. a leather belt
   C. snake sandals

8. What does Jerry's father give him when he gets out of prison?
   A. nintendo
   B. ten speed bike
   C. stereo

9. What is Jerry's father is prison for?
   A. stealing and stripping cars
   B. robbing a liquor store
   C. embezzling

10. What makes Grace look like a nerd, according to Jerry?
    A. bows in her hair
    B. her shoes
    C. her eyeglasses

FLIGHT #116 IS DOWN
Caroline B. Cooney

1. Where are Heidi's parents?
   A. overseas
   B. in the hospital
   C. on the plane

2. Who is the first volunteer on the scene?
   A. Ty
   B. Patrick
   C. Darriene

3. What is slowing down the rescue efforts?
   A. ice and snow
   B. rain and mud slide
   C. extreme heat and wind

4. What is the media calling the crash?
   A. The Dove Town Crash
   B. The Dove House Crash
   C. The Dove Creek Crash

5. Why did the plane crash?
   A. bomb
   B. bad weather
   C. doesn't say

6. Why can't the ambulances leave for the hospitals?
   A. snowdrift is in the way
   B. bridge is out
   C. one lane road is blocked with vehicles

7. What do Patrick and Heidi use for a bridge across the creek?
   A. door from a horse stall
   B. wing from the plane
   C. gate from the corral

8. What does Ty steal to help in the rescue?
   A. tools
   B. medical supplies
   C. school bus

9. What was kept in the barn?
   A. wounded
   B. dead bodies
   C. food for the victims and workers

10. Who died?
    A. Teddie
    B. Carly
    C. Darriene

FORWARD PASS

Thomas J. Dygard

1. What does Jill run plays as?
   A. tight end
   B. practice person only
   C. a decoy

2. How do the other members of the team feel about Jill?
   A. they accept her
   B. they ignore her
   C. they hate her

3. What would coach Frank Gardner not let his players do?
   A. be interviewed
   B. date
   C. play other sports

4. When does Jill's team find out about Jill playing with them?
   A. when they read the newspaper
   B. just before the first game
   C. at a press conference

5. How many times was Jill tackled?
   A. 2
   B. 5
   C. 0

6. Where does Jill dress for the home games?
   A. the girls' restroom
   B. the coach's office
   C. the girls' locker room

7. What does Jill do when it is time to sign up for basketball?
   A. she continues to play football
   B. she plays both football and basketball
   C. she quits the football team

8. Before the first game where do Jill and Scott practice passes?
   A. on the field
   B. in the gym
   C. at Scott's house

9. When does Frank first think about having Jill play football?
   A. during a girl's basketball game
   B. at a summer softball game
   C. over lunch with another coach

10. What do the students at Jill's school think about her playing on the football team?
    A. it's terrific
    B. it's awful
    C. they don't care

THE GHOST OF LOST ISLAND
Lisa Ketchum Murrow

1. What is Gabe afraid of?
   A. ghosts
   B. snakes
   C. the dark

2. What is Gabe's job during the sheep shearing?
   A. to jump on the wool
   B. to hold the sheep down
   C. to sack up the wool

3. Why does Delia fake her own death?
   A. her boyfriend dumped her
   B. she wanted to leave the farm
   C. she wanted to marry another man

4. What does Gabe find in the grapevine house?
   A. a diary
   B. a half eaten candy bar
   C. a picture of a maiden

5. What does Delia throw into the ocean?
   A. coins
   B. metal chest
   C. love letters

6. What does Grandpa want to do with Delia?
   A. marry her
   B. take her to a shelter
   C. help her find her family

7. Who finds the lamb?
   A. Gabe
   B. Ginny
   C. Delia

8. Who gets seasick?
   A. Gabe
   B. Ginny
   C. Grandpa

9. Where do Ginny and Gabe take Delia to help her escape?
   A. Murphy's Lookout
   B. the island reef
   C. the old farmstead

10. What sign does Delia leave to show she made it across the breakwater?
    A. red scarf on a pole
    B. milk can in the sand
    C. red scarf on the milk can

THE GIFT

Joan Lowery Nixon

1. What do leprechauns like?
   A. violin music
   B. a good trick
   C. a bowl of milk

2. Who does not believe in leprechauns?
   A. Aunt Nora
   B. Uncle Martin
   C. Grandpa

3. What does Brian catch at night on the porch?
   A. the cat
   B. a goose
   C. a fairy

4. Who does Brian think can read his mind?
   A. Nora
   B. animals
   C. leprechauns

5. Where does Granddad take Brian to see leprechauns?
   A. an abandoned farm
   B. a village wall
   C. an old castle

6. What is Brian afraid of?
   A. fairies
   B. Pookas
   C. leprechauns

7. What happens when Brian tries to catch a leprechaun in the barn?
   A. he lets the horses loose
   B. he falls asleep in the hay
   C. he falls down a ladder

8. What are the leprechauns doing when Brian finally sees them?
   A. counting their gold
   B. having a party
   C. playing a game of snooker

9. What does the leprechaun Brian takes home ask Brian to do for him?
   A. tie his shoes
   B. keep a secret
   C. keep him safe from the cat

10. When Brian shows the leprechaun to Granddad and Aunt Nora what does Aunt Nora see?
    A. a huge cat
    B. a leprechaun
    C. nothing

THE GIFT OF THE GIRL WHO COULDN'T HEAR
Susan Shreve

1. How long has Lucy been deaf?
   A. since birth
   B. since she was five
   C. one year

2. What part is Lucy trying out for?
   A. Annie
   B. orphan
   C. Molly

3. What is wrong with Eliza's house?
   A. it smells bad
   B. it is run down
   C. it is too small

4. What doesn't Lucy's mother allow her to do?
   A. go to a normal school
   B. learn to sign
   C. go out alone

5. What do Eliza and the musical's director give each other?
   A. bad advice
   B. corny jokes
   C. pretend cigarettes

6. Who does the director say is the best teacher in the school?
   A. Ms. Westfield
   B. Ms. Henderson
   C. Lucy Bressler

7. What happens when Lucy finishes auditioning?
   A. everyone stands and claps
   B. everyone boos
   C. there is dead silence

8. Who gets the role of Annie?
   A. Louisa Peale
   B. Sasha Brewer
   C. Eliza Westfield

9. What part does Lucy get?
   A. orphan
   B. stage manager
   C. Annie

10. Who signs Eliza's name to the tryout sheet?
    A. Mr. Blake
    B. Lucy
    C. Eliza

THE GIFT OF THE PIRATE QUEEN
Patricia Reilly Giff

1. What does Grace break that belongs to her teacher?
    A. glass bell
    B. coffee cup
    C. globe

2. What doesn't Fiona like?
    A. goats
    B. dogs
    C. horses

3. How does Grace's mother die?
    A. drown in the river
    B. plane crash
    C. fell down stairs

4. Why does no one like Lisa?
    A. she picks her nose
    B. she is dirty
    C. she curses

5. What does Grace do with the package with the bell in it?
    A. put an explanation in it
    B. put her card in it
    C. put Lisa's name on it

6. What had twins?
    A. Buddy
    B. Fiona
    C. Willie

7. What does Grace tell Amy at the hospital?
    A. I hate you
    B. I love you
    C. I wish you were home

8. What gift does Fiona give to Grace before Christmas?
    A. a pink crystal bell
    B. a doll that was Grace's mother's
    C. a picture of Grace's mother and Fiona

9. What gift does the pirate queen give to each family member?
    A. love
    B. courage
    C. unselfishness

10. What does Grace give Fiona for Christmas?
    A. a blue sweater
    B. her horse pictures
    C. a pair of earrings

THE GIRLFRIEND
R.L. Stine

1. How does Scotty describe Lora's parents?
   A. busybodies
   B. obnoxious
   C. generous

2. What attracts Scotty to Shannon?
   A. her flowing red hair
   B. her personality
   C. her wealth

3. What does Shannon do to hurt Scotty physically?
   A. break his hand
   B. punch him in the nose
   C. kick him in the shins

4. What is Ernie?
   A. horse
   B. snake
   C. mouse

5. How does Ernie die?
   A. poisoned
   B. run over
   C. cut in half

6. What does Scotty leave at Shannon's house?
   A. car
   B. Raider's cap
   C. school jacket

7. What does Shannon set on fire?
   A. Scotty's house
   B. Scotty's pet
   C. Scotty's car

8. How does Shannon hurt Lora?
   A. she puts ink on her dress
   B. she kills her cat
   C. she tells Lora about her and Scotty

9. What does Shannon call Scotty?
   A. her baby
   B. her hunk
   C. her stud muffin

10. Who does Shannon say she lives with?
    A. three brothers
    B. old maid aunt
    C. the chief of police

GOING FOR THE BIG ONE
P.J. Petersen

1. Why was Dave arrested?
   A. for being in a fight
   B. for being in possession of drugs
   C. for stealing a television

2. Why does the policeman shoot at Annie?
   A. she was stealing his patrol car
   B. she was helping Cracker escape
   C. she was shooting at him

3. What does Cracker pay Jeff and Dave to get out of his cabin?
   A. first aid kit
   B. rifle
   C. diamonds

4. What food is eaten on the trip across the mountains?
   A. fish and cereal
   B. spaghetti and oatmeal
   C. hamburgers and potatoes

5. Why did the men shoot Cracker?
   A. they thought he was a deer
   B. he was an escaped convict
   C. he stole their cocaine

6. What does Jeff kill for food?
   A. rabbit
   B. deer
   C. fish

7. Who jumps Cracker and gets the gun?
   A. Annie
   B. Jeff
   C. Dave

8. How much money do the three get for taking Cracker with them?
   A. $100
   B. $500
   C. $1,000

9. What does Annie throw away?
   A. bullets
   B. marijuana
   C. sleeping bag

10. Who does Cracker point his gun at and pull the trigger on?
    A. Annie
    B. Jeff
    C. Dave

GREENWITCH

Susan Cooper

1. What was stolen from Captain Toms?
   A. his dog, Rufus
   B. a map
   C. a wreath of leaves

2. Who is allowed to watch the making of the greenwitch?
   A. foreigners
   B. local girls
   C. everyone

3. What does Jane wish at the greenwitch ceremony?
   A. the greenwitch to be happy
   B. the grail to be found
   C. that the light overcomes the dark

4. What is the Dark disguised as?
   A. fisherman
   B. painter
   C. tourist

5. What does the painter steal from Barney?
   A. Barney's paints
   B. Barney's watch
   C. Barney's drawing

6. What is in the box in the painter's refrigerator?
   A. a chocolate cake
   B. a head
   C. the Cornish grail

7. What does the painter ask Barney to do?
   A. tell him what he sees inside the grail
   B. tell him why he drew the picture
   C. tell him where the manuscript is

8. What does the Greenwitch give to Jane?
   A. necklace
   B. wish
   C. manuscript

9. What do the boys find in an old barn?
   A. a book of magic spells
   B. the secret of the dark
   C. the Cornish grail

10. What does the painter live in?
    A. farm house
    B. gypsy caravan
    C. tent

HAIRLINE CRACKS
John Robert Taylor

1. What was Davis accused of?
   A. selling drugs
   B. stealing from the company
   C. breaking and entering

2. What does Witcham want to build?
   A. dam
   B. new town
   C. hospital

3. How is Iron-Face hurt?
   A. hit by a bull
   B. shot by Davis
   C. hit by a train

4. What do people call Witcham behind his back?
   A. Fuzzy
   B. Hairy
   C. Scar Face

5. How did Witcham get the scars on his head?
   A. surgery
   B. car accident
   C. fire

6. How does Witcham escape with Sam after seeing Sam's mother?
   A. in an armored car
   B. in a helicopter on the roof
   C. through the culvert in a dinghy

7. How does Witcham die?
   A. drown
   B. shoot out
   C. pushed out a 7th story window

8. What was Trubshaw going to do to Mo if Sam didn't answer Witcham's questions?
   A. kill her slowly
   B. beat her up with iron knuckles
   C. break her fingers with a wrench

9. Why was Sam in the hospital?
   A. he was shot
   B. he broke his collar bone
   C. he had a concussion

10. How did Sam find out he had to go to Simon's cottage?
    A. phone call
    B. post card
    C. Mo told him

HAS ANYONE SEEN ALLIE?

Hayden/Kistler

1. Where was Allie last seen?
   A. in a yellow Chrysler
   B. in a green pickup
   C. in a cattle stall

2. Who finds Allie's scarf?
   A. Cleata and Mike
   B. Steve and Judy
   C. Freddie and Jim

3. Where does Judy train Poppy?
   A. in the boulder field
   B. on the race track
   C. in an arena

4. Where does Steve find Allie's body?
   A. in a grave
   B. in a cave
   C. in the woods

5. Who does Judy like?
   A. Jim
   B. Freddie
   C. Steve

6. Where was Judy when she was shot by a coyote trap?
   A. in a ravine
   B. on the back porch
   C. at the mailbox

7. Who confessed to Allie's murder?
   A. Jim
   B. Mike
   C. Freddie

8. What was the terrible secret Allie knew about the murderer?
   A. he stole a champion horse
   B. he was an arsonist
   C. he killed a man in a hit and run accident

9. Who does Judy live with?
   A. Cleata
   B. Aunt Margaret
   C. Allie

10. Why does Judy want to follow Cleata into the canyon?
    A. so Judy wouldn't get lost in the dark
    B. because Cleata was ill
    C. she thinks Cleata killed Allie

HATCHET
Gary Paulsen

1. What caused the plane to crash?
    A. thunderstorm
    B. engine trouble
    C. pilot had a heart attack

2. What does Brian eat that makes him sick?
    A. gut berries
    B. bear
    C. beaver

3. What is Brian's secret?
    A. his mother kissed a strange man
    B. he likes living alone
    C. he didn't help the pilot out

4. What happened to Brian's leg?
    A. he broke it
    B. porcupine quills were in it
    C. it has poison ivy

5. What does Brian use for string for his bow?
    A. strips from his jacket
    B. thin piece of his belt
    C. his shoe string

6. How does Brian catch his first fish?
    A. his hands
    B. bow and arrow
    C. spear

7. Who steals Brian's turtle eggs?
    A. raccoon
    B. rat
    C. skunk

8. What does Brian eat first?
    A. eggs
    B. berries
    C. fish

9. What attacked Brian in the water?
    A. moose
    B. snake
    C. bear

10. What does the tornado do?
    A. cause the plane to surface
    B. cause Brian to become lost
    C. cause Brian to have a concussion

THE HAUNTING OF FRANCIS RAIN
Margaret Buffie

1. Who does Lizzie confide in about seeing ghosts on the island?
   A. Tim
   B. Evan
   C. Alex

2. Why does Lizzie decide Tim is an okay guy?
   A. he tries to rescue her in a boat
   B. he takes up for her against Evan
   C. he lets her do whatever she wants

3. Who gets along great with Tim?
   A. Erica
   B. Evan
   C. Lizzie

4. How many ghosts does Lizzie see?
   A. 3
   B. 5
   C. 7

5. What is wrong with Gran?
   A. asthma
   B. bronchitis
   C. her heart

6. Who do the eyeglasses Lizzie found belong to?
   A. Francis Rain
   B. Francis Rain's daughter
   C. Francis Rain's father

7. What do Lizzie and Alex find in an old rock ledge?
   A. eyeglasses
   B. an old Bible
   C. a sketch book

8. What advice does Lizzie give to her mother?
   A. divorce Tim
   B. go after Tim
   C. take her father back

9. Who does Lizzie learn is Francis Rain's daughter?
   A. her grandmother
   B. May Bird
   C. Alex's mother

10. What did the ghosts want Lizzie to let Francis Rain know?
    A. her daughter did not leave by choice
    B. they caught Francis Rain's killer
    C. her daughter was alive and well

HIGH TRAIL TO DANGER
Joan Lowery Nixon

1. What does Sarah and Susannah's uncle accuse them of knowing?
   A. where their father is
   B. stealing
   C. knowing their mother's secret hiding place

2. Who teaches Sarah to ride and shoot?
   A. Clint
   B. Jeremy
   C. Uncle Amos

3. Who holds up the train Sarah is on?
   A. Jesse James
   B. the Youngers
   C. Bell Star

4. What does Sarah do when she is being mugged?
   A. scream
   B. hit him with her umbrella
   C. give him her money

5. What does Sarah's father do for a living?
   A. mine gold
   B. rob trains
   C. gamble

6. What do the people who know Sarah's father tell her?
   A. he is dead
   B. go home
   C. they will give him the message

7. Where does Sarah find her father?
   A. in a boarding house
   B. in jail
   C. in a mine shack

8. Who does Sarah ask first about her father?
   A. Mrs. Fitch
   B. Lily
   C. Marshall Kelly

9. Where does Sarah keep her money?
   A. in her corset
   B. in her purse
   C. in her carpet bag

10. Who shoots the man who kills Sarah's father?
    A. Sarah
    B. Clint
    C. Marshall Kelly

HOOPS
Walter Dean Myers

1. Why doesn't Lonnie want Cal to be coach?
   A. he's a wino
   B. he's in the mob
   C. he's a terrible ball player

2. Who shot Lonnie's hand?
   A. Cal
   B. Lonnie
   C. Paul

3. What did Lonnie think when Cal didn't show up for the first game?
   A. Cal ripped off the uniform money
   B. Cal was in an accident
   C. Cal quit the ream

4. Why is Cal no longer playing pro ball?
   A. he had been injured
   B. he was caught shaving points
   C. he lost his game

5. What was Aggie's profession?
   A. hustler
   B. waitress
   C. singer

6. Why was Mary-Ann in the hospital?
   A. she was beat up
   B. she had her tonsils out
   C. she overdosed

7. What did Paul do that was illegal?
   A. steal welfare checks
   B. steal cars
   C. hustle pool

8. Why did Cal miss some of the games?
   A. he was in an accident
   B. he was kidnapped
   C. he was in jail

9. Who kills Cal?
   A. O'Donnell
   B. Tyrone
   C. Ugly

10. Who is Lonnie's girlfriend?
    A. Aggie
    B. Mary-Ann
    C. TJ

THE HOUSE ON HACKMAN'S HILL
Joan Lowery Nixon

1. Who used to live in the house on Hackman Hill?
   A. Mr. Karsten
   B. Jeff
   C. Debbie

2. Where does Paul live?
   A. in the basement
   B. in the tower room
   C. in the attic

3. What does Paul find?
   A. coin
   B. ring
   C. gold pin

4. What does the strange voice in the night call out?
   A. you'll be sorry
   B. where are my eyes
   C. you took my gold

5. Where does Paul hide the coin?
   A. in his room
   B. inside the VCR
   C. in a statue

6. What do they find with the mummy?
   A. the murder weapon
   B. gold
   C. Dr. Hackman's body

7. How do the kids escape the Anubis?
   A. trap door in the basement
   B. through a hidden passage
   C. through a fire escape

8. What happened to the mummy and Anubis?
   A. they were stolen
   B. they were vandalized
   C. they were burned up

9. Who is Anubis the guardian of?
   A. children
   B. the tombs
   C. women

10. What did Dr. Hackman want to turn his house into?
    A. hotel
    B. museum
    C. school

HOW COULD YOU DO IT, DIANE?
Stella Pevsner

1. Where does Max work?
   A. pawn shop
   B. bar
   C. drug store

2. Where did Diane get the glass she cut her arm from?
   A. a broken window
   B. picture frame
   C. broken mirror

3. How does Diane kill herself?
   A. overdose
   B. gun shot
   C. hangs herself

4. Why does Diane cut her arm?
   A. she wants to die
   B. to convince Max she loves him
   C. to scare her mom

5. What does Nell do after Diane dies?
   A. stops talking
   B. pretends Diane is still alive
   C. plays dead

6. Why does Bethany's Dad get angry at the psychiatrist's office?
   A. he blames himself
   B. he thinks everyone is lying to him
   C. he learns Diane had tried to kill herself before

7. Why does the school secretary come and get Bethany?
   A. to clean out Diane's locker
   B. to take her to the nurse
   C. to check her out of school

8. Where is the Halloween dance Bethany goes to?
   A. at the school
   B. at Max's home
   C. in a barn

9. Why does Diane kill herself?
   A. she was pregnant
   B. we don't know
   C. family problems

10. What was Bethany doing when she found Diane?
    A. cleaning the bathroom
    B. washing clothes
    C. bringing in the groceries

H.O.W.L. HIGH
Ellen Leroe

1. What tells Drac when something is about to happen?
   A. red magic dice
   B. his talking hat
   C. a magic pen

2. What is Drac's pet?
   A. a dragon
   B. a pigeon named Hawk
   C. a black cat

3. What did Rondo Orlac steal from Uncle Frederico?
   A. The Book of Shadows
   B. a magic cape
   C. the rope of death

4. What film did Drac give to a teacher to see?
   A. his gymnastics film
   B. Mandori going-away party
   C. his high school play

5. Who was Drac interviewed by?
   A. the school newspaper
   B. the 6 o'clock news
   C. Entertainment Now

6. What does Drac steal from Orlac's mansion?
   A. Orlac's old movies
   B. Orlac's statue
   C. Orlac's mask and ring

7. What did an evil shadow do for Drac?
   A. untie a knot
   B. cast a spell
   C. hide him

8. What is Lisa?
   A. a midget
   B. the class president
   C. a witch

9. What does Lisa own?
   A. a talking monkey
   B. magic scissors
   C. a golden ring

10. What causes Drac to see visions?
    A. a four leaf clover
    B. magic mirror glasses
    C. a magic potion

I KNOW WHAT YOU DID LAST SUMMER
Lois Duncan

1. What contest does Helen win?
   A. City History
   B. Miss Teen
   C. Golden Girl

2. Who was shot?
   A. Barry
   B. Julie
   C. Ray

3. Why is Mrs. Gregg in the hospital?
   A. nervous breakdown
   B. heart attack
   C. stabbed

4. Why does Barry's mother not approve of Helen?
   A. she's wealthy
   B. she dropped out of school
   C. she has a bad attitude

5. Who made an appointment to meet Barry at the athletic field?
   A. his girl
   B. his football coach
   C. a man with a photo

6. Who is Collie?
   A. Helen's brother
   B. Helen's neighbor
   C. Helen's boyfriend

7. Who is jealous of Helen?
   A. Bud
   B. Julie
   C. Elsa

8. Who tried to kill Barry, Helen and Julie?
   A. Megan
   B. Bud
   C. Elsa

9. How does Helen escape from Collie?
   A. by jumping through a window
   B. by blinding him with perfume
   C. by pushing him in the pool

10. Who saves Julie from being strangled?
    A. Ray
    B. Bud
    C. Barry

THE ICEBERG HERMIT
Arthur Roth

1. What did Allan's mother tell him to do?
   A. read his Bible daily
   B. marry Nancy
   C. become a whaler

2. Where did Allan get the scar on his arm?
   A. he fell down an iceberg
   B. he was bitten by a polar bear
   C. he was burned when the ship blew up

3. Where did Allan live for the first two years after the shipwreck?
   A. on the capsized ship
   B. on an island
   C. in a mountain cave

4. What did Allan name his pet?
   A. Tucker
   B. Nancy
   C. Smokey

5. How come the eskimos finally came and got Allan and took him home with them?
   A. Allan offered them money
   B. Allan overpowered them with his flintlock
   C. they recognized the words, 'Jesus Christ'

6. What do the eskimos not want Allan to do?
   A. help the women cook
   B. leave the camp
   C. help the men hunt

7. What does master Duff tell Allan's mother?
   A. Allan was lazy and stupid
   B. Allan should stay in school
   C. Allan should come and work for him

8. What job did Allan have before going to sea?
   A. he dug coal
   B. he was an errand boy
   C. he worked for a tailor

9. Who did Allan learn the eskimos he was living with really were?
   A. pirates
   B. descendants of the Norse Vikings
   C. Indians from India

10. How many years was Allan stranded before he was rescued by a whaling ship?
    A. 2
    B. 7
    C. 10

IN LANE THREE, ALEX ARCHER
Tessa Duder

1. What happens the first time Alex competes in a real swim meet?
   A. she wins
   B. she ties
   C. she knocks herself out

2. Besides swimming, what is Alex good at?
   A. ballet
   B. basketball
   C. running

3. How does Alex fracture her leg?
   A. playing hockey
   B. falling off her bike
   C. tripping at a dance

4. What part does Alex play in The Wizard of Oz?
   A. Scarecrow
   B. Tinman
   C. Dorothy

5. Who pays for Alex's lessons?
   A. Mr. Jack
   B. Andy
   C. Gram

6. What does Andy want to do?
   A. be a doctor
   B. go to sea
   C. be a swimming coach

7. How is Alex killed?
   A. drowns while sailing
   B. jumps off a bridge
   C. hit by a drunk driver

8. What does almost the whole town show up for?
   A. a rodeo
   B. a bridge walk
   C. a swim meet

9. What goes wrong at Alex's first dance?
   A. she breaks her shoe
   B. she falls while dancing
   C. she gets in a fight

10. What physical problem does Andy have?
    A. he stutters
    B. he limps
    C. he has epilepsy

IN OUR HOUSE SCOTT IS MY BROTHER

C.S. Adler

1. What does Jodi look like?
   A. a boy
   B. a movie star
   C. a sissy

2. What bad habit does Scott have?
   A. he spits
   B. he shoplifts
   C. he curses

3. What bad habit does Donna have?
   A. she drinks
   B. she lies
   C. she smokes

4. Where does Jodi's father bring everyone as a Christmas present?
   A. Hawaii
   B. snow skiing
   C. Europe

5. What does Jodi's dad say she can have for Christmas?
   A. new bedroom furniture
   B. a camera
   C. a puppy

6. What does everyone in Jodi's homeroom think she did?
   A. kiss Scott behind the bleachers
   B. break all the computers in the lab
   C. steal an African necklace

7. What is Scott good at?
   A. swimming
   B. dancing
   C. history

8. What does Mr. Briggs leave to the community in his will?
   A. his home
   B. money for a church building
   C. the glen

9. What does Scott give to Jodi for Christmas?
   A. a game
   B. a nature picture
   C. a necklace with feathers

10. What does Donna not allow anyone to eat?
    A. desserts
    B. meat
    C. snacks

IN THE FACE OF DANGER
Joan Lowery Nixon

1. What does Emma give to Megan?
   A. book
   B. penny
   C. puppy

2. Who dies from a rattlesnake bite?
   A. Lady
   B. Ben
   C. Farley

3. What does Mr. Cartwright give to Megan?
   A. a sketch of herself
   B. a silver dollar
   C. a wooden whistle

4. Why doesn't Ada Haskill like Megan?
   A. because Megan likes the prairie
   B. because Megan is Irish
   C. she doesn't like children

5. What does Emma read to Megan?
   A. the Bible
   B. the newspaper
   C. Aesop's fables

6. What kind of house does Farley have?
   A. sod
   B. dugout
   C. wood

7. What does Megan use to escape from the wolves?
   A. pitchfork
   B. gun
   C. fire

8. Who delivers Emma's baby?
   A. Ada
   B. Nelda
   C. Megan

9. Who captures the fugitive?
   A. Megan
   B. Farley
   C. Ben

10. What does Emma give Megan for Christmas?
    A. cloth doll
    B. new dress
    C. bonnet

THE INDIAN IN THE CUPBOARD
Lynne Reid Banks

1. What causes the cupboard to turn the Indian into a real person?
   A. magic words
   B. a special dance
   C. an old key

2. What else became real in the cupboard?
   A. a cowboy
   B. a dog
   C. a gunfighter

3. What did the white rat steal?
   A. a key
   B. a crayon
   C. a locket

4. What special talent does the cowboy have?
   A. he can sing
   B. he can draw
   C. he can write poetry

5. How does the cowboy get his nickname?
   A. he has a temper
   B. he tells jokes
   C. he cries easily

6. What kind of things can the cupboard make real?
   A. glass
   B. plastic
   C. metal

7. Who saves the cowboy's life?
   A. an Indian medicine man
   B. an Indian woman
   C. an army medic

8. Who sees the cowboy and Indian?
   A. Omri's parents
   B. the principal
   C. Omri's brothers

9. What does Omri do with the key in the end?
   A. gives it to his mother to keep
   B. throws it away
   C. hides it in the oak tree

10. What happens to the Indian chief when he sees Omri?
    A. he dies
    B. he laughs
    C. he attacks

INDIAN SUMMER
Barbara Girion

1. What do the Birdsong's have that they will not let Joni use?
   A. radio
   B. television
   C. phone

2. Where do Joni and Sarah sleep?
   A. loft
   B. trailer
   C. tepee

3. What does Joni find is missing when she returns from a walk with Sarah?
   A. Raggedy Ann
   B. bike
   C. necklace

4. Where does Chief Birdsong sleep?
   A. tepee
   B. trailer
   C. longhouse

5. What does Sarah give to Joni after telling her the story about how North America got it's Indian name?
   A. an Indian history book
   B. an Indian doll
   C. a turtle necklace

6. What is unusual about cornhusk dolls?
   A. they have no feet
   B. they have no face
   C. they have no arms

7. Who is the storyteller of the family?
   A. Chief Birdsong
   B. Joni
   C. Maw Maw

8. What Indian name does Sarah give to Joni?
   A. Joni Fire Hair
   B. Joni Bird Legs
   C. Joni with Tongue that Wags

9. What does Joni take in anger that belongs to Sarah?
   A. her wolf necklace
   B. her native dress
   C. her corn husk doll

10. What does Joni do that shocks everyone at the pow wow?
    A. she joins in one of the dances
    B. she beats on one of the drums
    C. she laughs at the Indians in their outfits

INTO THE DREAM

William Sleator

1. What is special about Paul and Francine?
   A. they are telepathic
   B. they have X-ray vision
   C. they can move things with their minds

2. What can Noah do?
   A. he can fly
   B. he can move things with thought
   C. he can crush steel with his hands

3. Who has been sending the dream messages to Paul and Francine?
   A. Cookie
   B. Jaleela
   C. Stardust

4. What causes Paul, Francine, Cookie, and Noah to have special powers?
   A. radiation
   B. beam from a UFO
   C. chemical treatment

5. How do Paul, Francine, Noah, and Cookie escape from Jaleela's apartment?
   A. service elevator
   B. back stairs
   C. fire escape

6. Who is chasing Paul, Francine, Noah, and Cookie?
   A. the police
   B. the mob
   C. the government agents

7. Where do paul, Francine, Noah, and Cookie run to?
   A. the subway
   B. the mall
   C. the train depot

8. Where do Paul, Francine, Noah, and Cookie go to hide?
   A. Wonderland Amusement Park
   B. the woods
   C. Chicago airport

9. What ride are Paul and Noah on when their seat breaks?
   A. roller coaster
   B. ferris wheel
   C. the tornado

10. What does Noah do when the seat breaks?
    A. climbs down the railing
    B. makes the seat float
    C. drops to his death

INVITATION TO THE GAME
Monica Hughes

1. How does the group get to Barton Oaks?
   A. plane
   B. bus
   C. subway train

2. Where does the group always find the invitations?
   A. inside the elevator
   B. taped to their wall
   C. in the mailbox

3. What happens at level one each time someone is about to get hurt?
   A. the game ends
   B. the danger disappears
   C. one of the group saves everyone

4. Why does the group choose the warehouse to live in?
   A. it is close to the hospital
   B. it is close to a library
   C. it is close to a park

5. Why is Rich added to the group of eight?
   A. they needed a farmer
   B. they needed a chemist
   C. they needed a doctor

6. Who is the last one to join the group?
   A. Trent
   B. Benta
   C. Scylla

7. What does the group not have access to because they are unemployed?
   A. bright colored clothes
   B. night entertainment
   C. newspapers

8. What is used for fishing line?
   A. vines
   B. Scylla's hair
   C. thread from clothes

9. What does the group name the new planet?
   A. Prize
   B. Invitation
   C. Peace

10. Where does the group go once a year to celebrate the anniversary of their arrival on the planet?
    A. to the mesa
    B. to the lake
    C. to the woods

IS ANYBODY THERE?

Eve Bunting

1. What does Marcus build his mother for Christmas?
   A. bike
   B. bookshelf
   C. bird cage

2. What was Marcus given that belonged to his father?
   A. car
   B. watch
   C. fishing rod

3. What was not stolen by the intruder?
   A. money and jewelry
   B. flashlight and clock
   C. sleeping bag

4. Where was the intruder living?
   A. garage
   B. attic
   C. park

5. What did Nick get for Christmas?
   A. wife
   B. necktie
   C. son

6. What did Marcus find in Nick's apartment?
   A. typewriter
   B. policeman
   C. his mother's picture

7. What does Nick have that makes Marcus upset?
   A. key to Marcus' house
   B. gun
   C. drugs

8. What does Anjelica wear for Christmas?
   A. Santa Claus suit
   B. red velvet dress with lace
   C. red and green lipstick

9. What is Nick good at?
   A. fishing
   B. photography
   C. telling stories

10. How does Blake find his father?
    A. address on a letter
    B. sees Nick on T.V.
    C. through a private detective

IS IT THEM OR IS IT ME?
Susan Haven

1. What does Billy teach Molly to do?
   A. forge their father's signature
   B. cut class
   C. disguise her voice

2. What does Molly's laugh sound like?
   A. screaming
   B. honking
   C. crying

3. What disease does Molly's mother have?
   A. breast cancer
   B. leukemia
   C. epilepsy

4. How many classes does Frack teach?
   A. 0
   B. 2
   C. 6

5. Who likes Molly?
   A. Billy
   B. Michael
   C. Derek

6. What does Mrs. Medina want Molly to do to her article on Frack?
   A. shorten it
   B. put more facts in
   C. leave out the opinions

7. What disgusting habit does Derek have?
   A. he belches
   B. he passes gas
   C. he picks his nose

8. What do all the social studies teachers force Frack to do?
   A. quit
   B. transfer
   C. teach

9. What does Derek like to play?
   A. tennis
   B. piano
   C. poker

10. Why does Billy get detention in Mr. Frack's classroom?
    A. for cutting Frack's class
    B. for hiding in the closet
    C. for cheating on Frack's test

THE ISLAND
Gary Paulsen

1. What does Brian's father not do well?
   A. farming
   B. read
   C. plumbing

2. What does Brian's father want to grow?
   A. berries
   B. wheat
   C. broccoli

3. What does Brian write in his notebook?
   A. what he observes and thinks about
   B. poetry about life
   C. his biography

4. What does Brian imitate?
   A. crow
   B. heron
   C. turtle

5. Where does Brian sleep while on the island?
   A. in a tent
   B. in a cave
   C. under a boat

6. Who does Brian paint?
   A. his mother and father
   B. his grandmother and Susan
   C. Ray and Susan's mother

7. What did Ray do that caused Brian to try to drown him?
   A. ruin Brian's painting
   B. hit Brian
   C. slap Susan

8. Who do Brian's parents send to the island?
   A. reporters
   B. professional counselor
   C. policemen

9. Who is spying on Brian?
   A. his father
   B. reporters
   C. social worker

10. Who does Brian invite out to the island after the T.V. crews leave?
    A. his father
    B. Susan's mother
    C. his mother

JEREMY THATCHER, DRAGON HATCHER
Bruce Coville

1. What kind of contest is Jeremy trying to win?
   A. writing contest
   B. checker contest
   C. art contest

2. What does Mary Lou want to do?
   A. kiss Jeremy
   B. chase Jeremy
   C. talk to Jeremy

3. When does the dragon go to sleep?
   A. when it drinks milk
   B. when it eats a girl
   C. when it is sung to

4. What must the egg have in order for it to hatch?
   A. warmth
   B. moonlight
   C. sunlight

5. What happens to Jeremy when he rides on the dragon's back?
   A. he becomes immortal
   B. he becomes invincible
   C. he becomes invisible

6. What does Jeremy do with the dragon's egg, teeth, and skin?
   A. burn them
   B. save them
   C. throw them away

7. What does the dragon, Tiamet, want to eat?
   A. Jeremy's sister
   B. Jeremy's dog
   C. Jeremy's gerbils

8. How do Jeremy and Tiamet communicate?
   A. with gestures
   B. through mental pictures
   C. through speaking

9. Where is Tiamet's home?
   A. in another world
   B. in Asia
   C. underground

10. Who decided Jeremy would hatch Tiamet?
    A. the dragon, itself
    B. Jeremy
    C. the store owner

JIM UGLY
Sid Fleischman

1. Why are people looking for Sam Brannon?
    A. he abandoned his son
    B. he broke out of jail
    C. he has stolen diamonds

2. What is Jim Ugly's real name?
    A. Amigo
    B. Jose
    C. Jimbo

3. What was buried in Sam Brannon's coffin?
    A. block ice
    B. potatoes
    C. dirt

4. Who shot Sam Brannon?
    A. Mr. Cornelius
    B. Yellow Leg
    C. Axie

5. What part does Jake play on stage?
    A. Romeo
    B. Robin Hood
    C. William Tell's son

6. Why is Wilhelmina angry with Sam?
    A. he forgot their anniversary
    B. he left her at the alter
    C. he stole her jewels

7. Who was going to use the diamonds to swindle people?
    A. Sam
    B. Axie
    C. Cornelius

8. How is D.D. Skeats hurt?
    A. a snake bite on the leg
    B. shot himself in the foot
    C. fell off a horse and broke his foot

9. Who lets Jake know his father is alive?
    A. Jim Ugly
    B. Axie
    C. Aurora

10. Where were the diamonds hidden?
    A. inside the chickens
    B. in the manure
    C. in the coffin

JUNGLERAMA
Vicki Grove

1. What do Mike and Easy win at the Wingding?
   A. stuffed bear
   B. nerf ball
   C. fish

2. Where does Easy live?
   A. tent
   B. cabin
   C. apartment

3. Who gives the boys a milk snake for their trailer?
   A. The Toytaker
   B. The Whiz
   C. the voodoo priest

4. What causes the town to lose its electricity?
   A. storm
   B. snakes on the wires
   C. sabotage

5. Who do the townspeople blame their bad luck on?
   A. Judd
   B. Jeremiah Harlan
   C. Mrs. Beason

6. What kind of animals does Judd raise?
   A. leopards and cheetahs
   B. unusual and exotic birds
   C. snakes and alligators

7. What do the men of the town do to Mrs. Beason?
   A. kill her cats
   B. run her out of town
   C. burn her house down

8. How do the boys get into Mrs. Beason's house to rescue her?
   A. roof
   B. tunnel
   C. window

9. Who kidnapped Cassie?
   A. her father
   B. Mrs. Beason
   C. Jeremiah Harlan

10. Why do the boys set off the Roman candle?
    A. to celebrate setting the animals free
    B. to celebrate Easy moving in with Mike's family
    C. to celebrate TJ's Dad getting a job

JUST A SUMMER ROMANCE
Ann M. Martin

1. When does Mel first see Justin?
   A. when Timmy hits him with a frisbee
   B. at the shopping center
   C. in New York City

2. Who is taking care of Justin while he is on Fire Island?
   A. mother
   B. housekeeper
   C. family friends

3. Why does Lacey not speak to Mel for 3 days?
   A. she is jealous of Mel's time with Justin
   B. she is away for the weekend
   C. she has been grounded

4. Why does everyone leave Fire Island early?
   A. to attend a big party
   B. hurricane Chester is coming
   C. to see the U.S. president in New York City

5. What does Mel learn about Justin from reading a magazine?
   A. he saved a boy from drowning
   B. he invented a way to recycle rubber
   C. he is the hot new t.v. star

6. Why doesn't Justin tell Mel who he really is?
   A. he is modest
   B. he doesn't trust her
   C. he doesn't want their relationship to change

7. What does Justin give Mel when he sees her at a benefit in New York City?
   A. his phone number
   B. a kiss
   C. his address

8. Where does Justin take Mel for a date in New York City?
   A. theater on Broadway
   B. the 21 Club
   C. Central Park Zoo

9. What does Justin give Mel on their date in New York City?
   A. necklace
   B. bag of sand
   C. stuffed bear

10. What does Justin catch Mel doing on the dunes?
    A. burying Timmy in the sand
    B. looking at him through binoculars
    C. flirting with another boy

KEVIN CORBETT EATS FLIES
Patricia Hermes

1. What does Bailey have for a pet?
    A. a green mouse
    B. a blue crab
    C. a green and black tarantula

2. Who does Bailey live with?
    A. her sister's family
    B. foster parents
    C. her grandparents

3. When Bailey and Kevin want to raise money for a dinner what do they do for practice?
    A. bathe a cat
    B. wash Kevin's father's car
    C. try different lemonade recipes

4. What does Kevin like to do?
    A. run
    B. write poems
    C. read

5. What do Kevin and Bailey ask Miss Holt permission to do?
    A. see the principal
    B. hold a pep rally
    C. write a school paper

6. Why were Miss Holt and Kevin's father laughing at dinner?
    A. Miss Holt was telling about the class
    B. Kevin's father was telling a joke
    C. the turkey was still frozen

7. When will Kevin and his father move to Oklahoma?
    A. when his father finds a new car
    B. when his father finds work
    C. when his father finds a new place to live

8. What does Bailey give to Kevin on the school steps just before he moves?
    A. her address
    B. a handshake
    C. a poem she wrote

9. What does Miss Holt want to do with the money Kevin and Bailey make?
    A. let Kevin and Bailey keep it
    B. put it in the class treasury
    C. split it equally among and the five who earned it

10. How often do Kevin and his father move?
    A. about once a year
    B. about every six months
    C. about every two years

A KILLING FREEZE
Lynn Hall

1. What did Mrs. Amling do for a living?
   A. teach creative dance
   B. clean houses
   C. write children's books

2. What were all the visitors in town for?
   A. winterfest
   B. a carnival
   C. the county fair

3. Where is the second murder victim found?
   A. frozen inside a block of ice
   B. on the snowmobile trail
   C. inside a snowman

4. What does Clarie's father do for a living?
   A. cut and sell firewood
   B. sell skis and snowmobiles
   C. ski instructor

5. How does someone overhear Clarie's conversation with her father about who the murderer might be?
   A. listened through the window by the bushes
   B. hid in the back room of the store
   C. listened down the chimney pipe on the roof

6. What does Clarie learn about Mrs. Amling that she didn't know?
   A. she had been married
   B. she had a son
   C. she was in hiding

7. Who does Clarie think looks like the kid in the picture?
   A. her father
   B. Rat Proctor
   C. the sheriff, Keith

8. What killed Mrs. Amling?
   A. a knife wound
   B. a falling icicle
   C. a wooden stake

9. Who killed Mr. Moline?
   A. Bernie Rodas
   B. Keith
   C. Ray Proctor

10. What happened to Clarie's mother when Clarie was born?
    A. she ran away
    B. she died
    C. she married Clarie's father

A KIND OF THIEF

Vivien Alcock

1. Where does Sophia go when her husband is arrested?
   A. Italy
   B. America
   C. Brazil

2. Who is a foster child?
   A. Matthew
   B. Timmons
   C. Judy

3. What does Ellinor's father think of his relatives?
   A. they're dull and boring
   B. they're exciting
   C. they're too generous

4. Where does Timmons take Ellinor and lock her up?
   A. in the attic of their house
   B. old house in the woods
   C. in the barn

5. What does Timmons as a young boy promise Mrs. Carter?
   A. that he'd never lie again
   B. that he'd never cut school again
   C. that he'd never steal again

6. Where does Ellinor hide the money so Timmons won't find it?
   A. in the flower bed
   B. in the pantry
   C. in Mrs. Carter's room

7. Who runs away?
   A. Matthew
   B. Judy
   C. Ellinor

8. Who gets hurt when the tree falls through the house in the woods?
   A. Matthew
   B. Timmons
   C. Ellinor

9. Who does Ellinor give the money to?
   A. Timmons
   B. Mrs. Castle
   C. Sophia

10. What does Ellinor tell Sophia she did with the receipt?
    A. lost it
    B. burned it
    C. threw it away

KISSES

Judith Caseley

1. What does Hannah think about her blind date with Lance?
   A. it was great
   B. it was okay
   C. it was terrible

2. Who has a crush on Hannah?
   A. George
   B. Lance
   C. Richard

3. What does Hannah give her speech on?
   A. how to play the violin
   B. how to apply makeup
   C. how to train a dog

4. Who does Hannah have a crush on?
   A. George
   B. Richard
   C. Lance

5. Who dies?
   A. Hannah's brother
   B. Richard
   C. Hannah's grandfather

6. What did Mr. Kreutzer do at Hannah's violin lesson?
   A. give her a gift
   B. molest her
   C. hit her

7. What does Bobby teach Hannah how to do?
   A. swim
   B. dance
   C. ice skate

8. What do Deidre's parents do a lot of?
   A. go out of town
   B. fight
   C. make speeches

9. What did Uncle Joe do that Grandpa couldn't forgive?
   A. marry someone who wasn't Jewish
   B. leave the family business
   C. refuse to fight in the war

10. What does Bobby Mack send to Hannah?
    A. unsigned poems
    B. flowers
    C. candy

LEAVE THE COOKING TO ME
Judie Angell

1. What does Shirley Merton's mother think Shirley is doing?
   A. selling drugs
   B. catering
   C. shoplifting

2. What does Mrs. Merton find in Evelyn's room?
   A. food
   B. white powder
   C. list of names and a gun

3. How does Shirley get the food to the homes of the customers?
   A. she drives
   B. she hires a van and driver
   C. Terry drives them

4. To keep Shirley's secret what does Evelyn make Shirley do for her?
   A. buy her a new dress
   B. cater a party just for her
   C. clean the house for a month

5. What does Jim Fiske help Mrs. Merton do?
   A. follow Shirley
   B. catch some drug dealers
   C. questions some kids about Vanessa

6. What does Shirley cater?
   A. breakfasts
   B. dinners
   C. lunches

7. What happens at the last catering job of the season?
   A. Terry drops the turkey
   B. Shirley runs out of food
   C. Mary Kay doesn't show up

8. What is Terry secretly doing?
   A. stealing money from the catering service
   B. starting his own business
   C. learning to cook all of Shirley's recipes

9. Where is Evelyn while Shirley is doing her catering?
   A. at her grandparents
   B. at summer camp
   C. in summer school

10. What does Evelyn tell Shirley about catering?
    A. that Vanessa does not have to go to all the jobs
    B. that she doesn't have to pay the help
    C. that Shirley needs to advertise with flyers

LIBBY ON WEDNESDAY
Zilpha Keatley Snyder

1. Where does Libby go to be alone?
   A. tree house
   B. bedroom
   C. gazebo

2. What do Libby's classmates call her?
   A. McMuffin
   B. McBrain
   C. McFlat

3. Who lives in the Graham McCall house and is not related to Libby?
   A. Elliott
   B. Gillian
   C. Christopher

4. What is Libby's hobby?
   A. writing songs
   B. collecting 30's stuff
   C. collecting bugs

5. What is physically wrong with Alex?
   A. has only half his left foot
   B. his mouth is twisted
   C. cerebral palsy

6. Why is Mizzo no longer sponsoring the writer's workshop?
   A. she was transferred
   B. she got married and quit
   C. she is in the hospital

7. Why does G.G.'s dad beat him up?
   A. the dad is drunk
   B. he failed math
   C. he came home late

8. Who does Libby write to?
   A. Cordelia
   B. Gillian
   C. Mercedes

9. What is Alex's nickname?
   A. The Clutz
   B. The Great
   C. The Brain

10. What do the members of the FFW think G.G. is?
    A. clumsy
    B. scared
    C. brave

THE LIFEGUARD
Richie Tankersley Cusick

1. What does Kelsey find in her room that shows someone has been in there?
   A. seaweed
   B. mud
   C. wet towel

2. What does Kelsey learn about Neale?
   A. he was in prison
   B. he was in a mental institution
   C. he was an addict

3. What does Kelsey find in Isaac's home?
   A. Beth's red scarf
   B. Beth's shoes
   C. Beth's body

4. Where does Kelsey go that she is not supposed to go?
   A. into an abandoned shack
   B. into a lighthouse
   C. into Skip's house

5. Why is Kelsey afraid of the water?
   A. she can't swim
   B. because the water has sharks
   C. because her father drowned

6. Who is killing the girls?
   A. Skip
   B. Neale
   C. Justin

7. What causes Skip and Kelsey to have a wreck in the storm?
   A. flat tire
   B. can't see and go over the cliff
   C. run over Isaac's body

8. Why does the killer attack Donna?
   A. he thinks she is Kelsey
   B. Donna knows who is doing the killing
   C. she is female

9. What happens to Donna?
   A. she is killed
   B. she breaks her leg
   C. she is bit by a shark

10. Where do Neale and Skip find Donna, Kelsey, and Beth?
    A. in the ocean
    B. in a cave under the lighthouse
    C. on the rocks of the cliffs

LISA'S WAR
Carol Matas

1. What does Lisa do to two German soldiers on a streetcar?
   A. laugh at them
   B. threaten them
   C. throw up on them

2. How many days a week do children go to school?
   A. 2-3 days
   B. 6 days
   C. 0 days

3. What does Lisa leave on the streetcar?
   A. underground newspapers
   B. her coat
   C. her school books

4. What does Susanne stop doing after her parents are killed?
   A. eating
   B. talking
   C. playing

5. What is hidden under the floorboards of Susanne's closet?
   A. money
   B. food
   C. guns

6. Where do Lisa's family and friends hide?
   A. underground
   B. in the hospital
   C. at the school

7. How do the Dane's escape to Sweden?
   A. by train
   B. by plane
   C. by fishing boat

8. How do the Dane's get to the waterfront?
   A. horse
   B. ambulance and taxi
   C. train and bus

9. What do they do to the children to keep them quiet?
   A. drug them
   B. feed them
   C. sing to them

10. What happens when Lisa and Stepan are in the rowboat?
    A. it sinks
    B. they get shot
    C. they get lost

LOSING JOE'S PLACE
Gordon Korman

1. What kind of job do the boys get?
   A. making plastic bubble blowers
   B. being errand boys for engineers
   C. working in the public library

2. What happens the first day in Joe's apartment?
   A. the stove catches on fire
   B. one falls through the stairs
   C. they break a window

3. What happens after one week on the job?
   A. they get raises
   B. two of them are fired
   C. they quit

4. What happened to Joe's camero the first week?
   A. it was wrecked
   B. it was stolen
   C. it was vandalized

5. Why were Don and Jason arrested?
   A. drunk driving
   B. shoplifting
   C. stealing Joe's car

6. What does Rootbeer take a picture of?
   A. his thumb
   B. a bread crumb
   C. a cockroach

7. How does Rootbeer get the rent money?
   A. by wrestling pros
   B. by robbing a liquor store
   C. by getting a job

8. What broke the diner's window?
   A. people in a fight
   B. a car
   C. a flying hubcap

9. What does Jason do while Plotnick is in the hospital?
   A. he throws a wild party
   B. he runs the diner
   C. he lets his friends eat free

10. What does Jason rename the diner?
    A. A Taste of Paris
    B. Chocolate Memories
    C. The Sweet Tooth

LOST BOYS NEVER SAY DIE
Alan Brown

1. Why is Frances Rupert in the woods at night?
   A. to sneak a smoke
   B. to meet her boyfriend
   C. to hide from Flynn

2. What does Lewis lose in the woods?
   A. his dog
   B. his treasure map
   C. his way home

3. Why does Lewis leave the train?
   A. Flynn is on it
   B. to get something to eat
   C. to buy a magazine

4. What happens to Lewis as he is spying on Max in the woods?
   A. he sneezes
   B. he falls out of a tree
   C. he is stung by a bee

5. What does Max ask Lewis for?
   A. flashlight
   B. money
   C. can opener

6. What does Max use in the dishwasher and washing machine for soap?
   A. shampoo
   B. bubble bath
   C. powdered milk

7. When Lewis gets sick who does he call?
   A. Betsy
   B. Frances Rupert
   C. Flynn

8. Who does Betsy pretend to be when she and Lewis have dinner with the Ruperts?
   A. Lewis's aunt
   B. Lewis's cousin
   C. Lewis's grandmother

9. Why was Flynn taken to the hospital?
   A. he was unconscious
   B. he broke his collar bone
   C. he broke his leg

10. What did Flynn do to be arrested?
    A. beat up Lewis
    B. wreck the theater
    C. steal the props

LOST IN THE BARRENS
Farley Mowat

1. What were Awasin and Jamie going to see when they crashed their canoe?
   - A. stone house
   - B. gold mine
   - C. penguins

2. Why do Awasin and Jamie go to the Chipeweyan camp?
   - A. to raid their village
   - B. to see if they were starving
   - C. to visit Awasin's grandmother

3. Who are the Chipeweyans scared of?
   - A. Eskimos
   - B. Vikings
   - C. white men

4. Who's grave does Jamie rob?
   - A. Eskimo
   - B. Viking
   - C. miner

5. What do Awasin and Jamie not eat?
   - A. berries
   - B. caribou
   - C. nuts

6. What is the Killing Place?
   - A. where a great battle was fought
   - B. where human sacrifices were held
   - C. where the caribou are killed

7. What do Awasin and Jamie have for a pet?
   - A. fawn
   - B. dog
   - C. moose

8. Who is part Eskimo and part white?
   - A. Jamie
   - B. Awasin
   - C. Peetyuk

9. Who is hurt in the bear attack?
   - A. Peetyuk
   - B. Ayuskemmo
   - C. Awasin

10. Who adopts Peetyuk?
    - A. Ayuskemmo
    - B. Pete's uncle
    - C. the Chipeweyan chief

LYDDIE
Katherine Paterson

1. What does Lyddie do with the calf money?
   A. give it to a runaway slave
   B. bury it
   C. put it in the bank

2. How does Lyddie ruin her clothes?
   A. ripped getting away from Mr. Marsden
   B. pushing a stagecoach out of the mud
   C. rescuing a child from being run down

3. Who finds Lyddie a place to live?
   A. stage driver
   B. her uncle
   C. Luke

4. What does Lyddie buy with her savings?
   A. hat with a plume
   B. book
   C. candies

5. What does the factory require the girls to do?
   A. not get married
   B. stay away from liquor
   C. attend church

6. What are the workers asking for in the petition?
   A. Sundays off
   B. better wages
   C. 10 hour work day

7. Where does Lyddie's mother die?
   A. insane asylum
   B. farm
   C. hospital

8. Why is Lyddie fired?
   A. late too often
   B. works too slow
   C. moral turpitude

9. Who wants to marry Lyddie?
   A. Charlie
   B. Luke
   C. Mr. Marsden

10. What does Lyddie decide to do after she is fired?
    A. buy a farm
    B. go to college
    C. get married

MAGGIE, TOO

Joan Lowery Nixon

1. What is Flowerpot?
   A. cat
   B. parrot
   C. dog

2. What does Margaret have to do her first day in Houston?
   A. babysit two-year-olds
   B. chores
   C. run errands

3. What does everyone tell Margaret she has?
   A. a sense of humor
   B. a temper
   C. the measles

4. Who is Margaret named after?
   A. her mother
   B. her grandmother
   C. her aunt

5. Why does Margaret climb through her grandmother's second story window?
   A. to sneak off to the post office
   B. to hide in her room
   C. to unlock the bathroom door

6. What is stuck to Margaret's sneakers?
   A. gum
   B. toilet paper
   C. grass and clay

7. What does Margaret's grandmother give to her?
   A. a framed picture of her mother
   B. her mother's favorite book
   C. a scrapbook of her mother

8. Who is the only one that can make Flowerpot behave?
   A. Dennis
   B. Gloria
   C. Margaret

9. What does Margaret Landry win?
   A. kite
   B. trip to Cancun
   C. record collection

10. How does Margaret save her grandmother from Mr. Bubba Gletz?
    A. poured hot coffee on him
    B. hit him with a flower vase
    C. kicked him with a karate kick

THE MAN FROM THE OTHER SIDE
Uri Orlev

1. What nationality was Marek's real father?
   A. Jewish
   B. German
   C. Polish

2. What does the family take away from Marek's grandfather after he eats each day?
   A. dinner knife
   B. false teeth
   C. wine bottle

3. Where does Marek work?
   A. tavern
   B. tailor shop
   C butcher shop

4. What does Antony do every Sunday evening?
   A. play poker
   B. get drunk
   C. go to Mass

5. What does Marek's grandmother sell?
   A. candy
   B. fruit
   C. cigarettes

6. How is Marek trapped in the Jewish ghetto?
   A. he is locked in a bomb shelter
   B. he broke his leg and can't walk out
   C. the sewer blew up

7. Who is killed in the fighting?
   A. Pan Jozek
   B. Marek
   C. Antony

8. Who is wounded helping the Jews to escape?
   A. Marek
   B. Marek's real father
   C. Antony

9. What is wrong with Marek's grandfather?
   A. he is losing his sight
   B. he has a confused mind
   C. he has the palsy

10. What question does Antony ask Marek?
    A. if he can adopt him
    B. if he can marry his mother
    C. if he wants a little brother

MANIAC MAGEE
Jerry Spinelli

1. What does Maniac carry everywhere?
    A. Amanda's book
    B. stuffed bear
    C. switchblade

2. Who does Maniac live with?
    A. his teacher
    B. Amanda's family
    C. his father

3. What does Amanda carry in her suitcase?
    A. her library
    B. her clothes
    C. her toys

4. When Maniac plays baseball with McNab what is used for a ball?
    A. orange
    B. frog
    C. golf ball

5. What does Maniac like to run on?
    A. track
    B. roof tops
    C. the rails

6. What is Maniac allergic to?
    A. spinach
    B. peanut butter
    C. pizza

7. What does Maniac do to win a year's supply of free pizza?
    A. untie a knot
    B. color a picture
    C. have his name drawn

8. Where does Maniac live whenever he's on his own?
    A. in the park
    B. in an alley
    C. at the zoo

9. What was Earl Grayson's former occupation?
    A. elephant trainer
    B. minor league pitcher
    C. olympic trainer

10. What does Maniac teach Grayson how to do?
    A. play poker
    B. read
    C. make a sloppy joe

MAX AND ME AND THE TIME MACHINE
Greer and Ruddick

1. What causes Sir Bevis's horse to throw him in the match?
   A. Max yelled Geronimo
   B. the horse was run through with the lance
   C. the horse tripped

2. How long does Steve think he reset the time machine for?
   A. one week
   B. eight hours
   C. five days

3. What does Lady Elizabeth do when Steve wins the jousting match?
   A. tie a white scarf on his lance
   B. extend her hand for a kiss
   C. throw Steve a gold piece

4. Who romances Lady Elizabeth at the hunt for Steve?
   A. Agnes
   B. Max
   C. Hampshire Mauler

5. What advice does everyone keep asking Steve about while on the hunt?
   A. deer
   B. sword fighting
   C. falcons

6. Why does everyone laugh at Sir Bevis as they return to the castle?
   A. he is covered with manure
   B. he is riding backwards
   C. he is pushed into the moat

7. When Max leaves the body of the horse who does he become?
   A. Squire Niles
   B. Lady Elizabeth
   C. Hampshire Mauler

8. What does the Earl of Hampshire want Steve to do?
   A. marry Elizabeth
   B. stay away from his family
   C. join the crusades

9. Where is Dr. Gathergood's laboratory?
   A. in the tower
   B. in the dungeon
   C. in the cave

10. What does Sir Bevis accuse Steve of?
    A. casting a magic spell on his horse
    B. stealing his great great grandfather's ear
    C. having offensive eating habits

MAX AND ME AND THE WILD WEST
Greer and Ruddick

1. Why does the train conductor want to have Wilbur McNabb arrested?
   A. for cheating at cards
   B. for stealing his wallet
   C. for ruining Steve's hair

2. Who does Steve materialize as?
   A. an actor
   B. an outlaw
   C. a sheriff

3. What is Luke Plummer's nickname?
   A. Tumbleweed Kid
   B. Jack Rabbit Jumper
   C. Lariat Luke

4. What does Wilbur McNabb sell to a cowboy?
   A. a love potion
   B. jumping shoes
   C. a coffee pot

5. What does Jr. Sitwell do every time he sees Steve?
   A. laugh
   B. runaway
   C. shoot him with a pea shooter

6. What is Max's hobby?
   A. trick riding on a horse
   B. magic tricks
   C. telling stories

7. What does Gentleman John Hooten's partner wear for a disguise?
   A. a bandana
   B. women's hose
   C. flour sack

8. Why was Gentleman John Hooten going to kidnap Max?
   A. to hold Max ransom
   B. so Max would write a story about him
   C. to get advice about his poems

9. Who does Steve have a secret meeting with his first day in Silver Gulch?
   A. the sheriff
   B. Gentleman John Hooten
   C. Luke Plummer

10. What is in the box that's on stage?
    A. chicken
    B. hat
    C. snake

THE MIND TRAP
G. Clifton Wisler

1. What surgery do the students all have done to them?
   A. exploratory brain surgery
   B. mind control surgery
   C. implant surgery

2. Who gets miraculously healed at the hospital?
   A. Scott
   B. David
   C. Tiaf

3. Where does Malin take the students for a field trip?
   A. Egyptian museum
   B. Ranger baseball game
   C. Dallas zoo

4. What gives Scott a headache whenever he is near it?
   A. room 12
   B. outer wall
   C. Dr. Edgefield's office

5. What does Dr. Edgefield search all new students for?
   A. deformed toes
   B. mutated bone structure
   C. clover leaf birthmark

6. What is Scott not able to do inside the institute that he can do outside?
   A. heal people
   B. communicate with Tiaf
   C. read thoughts

7. What does Scott's ring do?
   A. protect him from danger
   B. send homing signals
   C. amplify energy

8. What diversion do the students make in order to escape?
   A. they set off the burglar alarms
   B. they start a fire
   C. they start a fight

9. How many people has Dr. Edgefield killed?
   A. three
   B. five
   C. seven

10. Where does Tiaf take the children?
    A. colony in Oregon
    B. Zhypos
    C. Antrian star system

MONKEY SEE, MONKEY DO
Barthe Declements

1. What is unusual about Clayton?
    A. he has purple hair
    B. he has a ponytail
    C. he has no hair

2. What does Jerry take on Wednesday's after school?
    A. piano lessons
    B. gymnastics
    C. swimming lessons

3. What does Grace get kicked out of?
    A. church choir
    B. restaurant
    C. car pool

4. Why is Jerry sent home from school?
    A. he is sick
    B. he was in a fight
    C. he was dressed inappropriately

5. What kind of job does Jerry's dad get fired from?
    A. editing magazine articles
    B. repairing phone lines
    C. selling appliances

6. What does Jerry help his dad fix up?
    A. Trans Am
    B. Mustang
    C. Camaro

7. What does Jerry do to try to keep his dad from committing a crime?
    A. jump out of his tree house
    B. sabotage his dad's car
    C. tell Grace's father

8. Where does Jerry ask his dad to take his friends?
    A. to the mall
    B. to the zoo
    C. to the T.V. station

9. What does Jerry's dad get arrested for?
    A. drunken and disorderly conduct
    B. shoplifting cigarettes
    C. hit and run

10. What does Jerry try out for?
    A. basketball team
    B. class play
    C. musical

THE MONSTER GARDEN
Vivien Alcock

1. What does Frankie name the monster?
   A. Betty
   B. Hattie
   C. Monnie

2. Who does not like the monster?
   A. Julia
   B. David
   C. Monnie

3. What does Julia give to Frankie?
   A. notebook
   B. camera
   C. scales

4. How long does Frankie tell her friends she is going to keep the monster?
   A. forever
   B. eight days
   C. two years

5. Who is Alf?
   A. the neighbor
   B. the housekeeper
   C. the gardener

6. Where does Monnie live?
   A. fish tank
   B. rabbit hutch
   C. bird cage

7. When Monnie escapes where does Frankie find it?
   A. in a tree
   B. on the roof
   C. neighbor's pond

8. Who did not keep the secret?
   A. John
   B. Julia
   C. Alf

9. Where did John take Monnie and Frankie to hide?
   A. his dad's lumber yard
   B. tool shed
   C. his bedroom closet

10. Who keeps Frankie from drowning?
    A. Monnie
    B. Frankie's dad
    C. John

THE MONUMENT
Gary Paulsen

1. How did Rocky get her nickname?
   A. she collected rocks
   B. she likes Silvester Stallone
   C. she threw rocks

2. What do Emma and Fred do a lot of?
   A. drink
   B. kiss
   C. fight

3. Where did Rocky live before she was nine?
   A. in an orphanage
   B. with her parents
   C. in a hospital

4. Who is Python?
   A. Rocky's boyfriend
   B. Rocky's dog
   C. a local farmer

5. What did Rocky think Mick was when she first saw him?
   A. bum
   B. body builder
   C. pervert

6. What is the present Mick gives to Rocky?
   A. a set of drawing pencils
   B. an art book
   C. a paint set

7. What happens to Mick in the Weak Beer Emporium?
   A. he is asked to draw pictures of the men
   B. he gets drunk
   C. he gets beat up

8. What happened in the courtroom to Mick's pictures?
   A. they were sold
   B. they were wadded up
   C. they were given away

9. What kind of monument did the town get?
   A. trees
   B. statue
   C. wall of names

10. Why is Mrs. Landon angry with the picture Mick drew of her?
    A. she is nude
    B. she looks old
    C. she looks ugly

THE MOON BY NIGHT
Madeleine L'Engle

1. What does Zachary always talk about?
   A. doomsday
   B. religion
   C. conservation

2. Why is Vicky's dad concerned about Zachary?
   A. he appears to be all alone
   B. he has a heart condition
   C. he has no ambition

3. What is Vicky's dad?
   A. doctor
   B. preacher
   C. lawyer

4. Where does Vicky learn about prejudice against Americans?
   A. England
   B. Canada
   C. Mexico

5. How does Vicky feel when she's around Zachary?
   A. happy
   B. grown up
   C. frightened

6. Where does Vicky meet Andy?
   A. at the hospital
   B. Grand Tetons
   C. Yellowstone National Park

7. What does Andy save Jo Lee from?
   A. bear
   B. leopard
   C. snake

8. What does Vicky think about after meeting Zachary?
   A. patriotism
   B. death
   C. God being fair

9. Why couldn't Vicky climb back over the mountain at Black Ram?
   A. she had broken her leg
   B. the mountain had fallen
   C. it was too dark

10. Where was Zachary rescued from?
    A. tree
    B. cave
    C. creek

MORE THAN MEETS THE EYE
Jeanne Betancourt

1. What reminds Dary of the killings in Cambodia?
    A. the evening news
    B. seeing the American soldiers
    C. Brad Mulville's green truck

2. How does Dary let Liz know about her family being killed in Cambodia?
    A. by painting a picture
    B. she tells her
    C. by writing a story

3. What does Ben tell his parents he is doing when he is really going on a date with Liz?
    A. studying at the library
    B. working on a school project at Brad's
    C. helping Mr. Tayback

4. What is Dary allergic to?
    A. penicillin
    B. milk
    C. bee stings

5. What does Ben do when a racist remark is made in class?
    A. he gets in a fight
    B. he ignores it
    C. he walks out of class

6. Who volunteers to help the two Koreans at school?
    A. Ben
    B. Brad
    C. Liz

7. How does the business community feel about the Koreans?
    A. they welcome them
    B. they try to scare them away
    C. they are afraid of them

8. What will Brad's boss do if Brad defends the Koreans?
    A. give his a raise
    B. fire him
    C. cut his hours

9. How long do the Koreans want to keep their store open?
    A. 24 hours, 7 days a week
    B. 9 a.m. to 6 p.m., Monday through Saturday
    C. 6 a.m. to midnight, 7 days a week

10. What does Brad accuse Ben of?
    A. giving him a flat tire
    B. calling him and hanging up
    C. starting a rumor about him

MOUSE RAP

Walter Dean Myers

1. What does Beverly do to Bobby?
   A. kiss him
   B. tell on him
   C. beat him up

2. Who did Grampa formerly work for?
   A. Tiger Moran
   B. the police
   C. Dr. Baker

3. Who beats Mouse at basketball?
   A. a monkey
   B. a girl
   C. his father

4. Who is Mr. D?
   A. Mouse's teacher
   B. Mouse's father
   C. a detective

5. What does the guy have who fights Mouse?
   A. gun
   B. lead pipe
   C. artificial leg

6. Where in the bank is Booster's gun hidden?
   A. under the counter
   B. in the umbrella stand
   C. in a potted plant

7. What did Booster's grandmother teach him to do?
   A. obey the law
   B. gamble
   C. pick pockets

8. Where does the gang find the hidden treasure?
   A. in a hole
   B. in a desk
   C. in a closet

9. What does Beverly get for a pet?
   A. snake
   B. hamster
   C. rabbit

10. What place do they come in at the dance contest?
    A. second
    B. fifth
    C. first

THE MOZART SEASON
Virginia Euwer Wolff

1. What does Mr. Trouble do at all the concerts?
   A. dance
   B. fight
   C. conduct

2. What is Allegra's job?
   A. set up the stage
   B. page turner
   C. record the performance

3. What happened to Karen who was supposed to play the Mozart Concerto in the park?
   A. broken fingers
   B. flu
   C. she ran away

4. Who is Allegra's teacher?
   A. Mr. Landauer
   B. Mr. Kaplan
   C. Bubbe Rassa

5. Where does Deirdre drop her earring?
   A. in the drainage ditch
   B. in the gerbil cage
   C. in a cello

6. What was the gift Allegra's grandmother sent to her?
   A. pearl sweater
   B. China doll
   C. velvet purse

7. What happened to the six finalists at the television studio?
   A. stuck in an elevator
   B. in a fire
   C. in a hold up

8. What is the name of Allegra's cat?
   A. Sophy
   B. Symphony
   C. Heavenly Days

9. What does Allegra's mother say everything is?
   A. fate
   B. a matter of life or death
   C. no big deal

10. How does Allegra do in the competition?
    A. she comes in first
    B. she doesn't place
    C. she comes in third

MURDER IN A PIG'S EYE
Lynn Hall

1. What does Henry Siler eat in the house that his wife has forbidden him to eat?
   A. chocolates
   B. greasy bacon
   C. red licorice

2. What does Bodie's mother want to become?
   A. stand up comedienne
   B. champion barrel racer
   C. veterinarian

3. What is Gloria?
   A. pig
   B. stallion
   C. dog

4. What does Gracie do on Henry's farm?
   A. clean his house
   B. sit on Beauty and read
   C. train his horses

5. What does Bodie's father do?
   A. plumber
   B. sheriff
   C. newspaper man

6. What does Bodie find in the pig pen?
   A. a woman's glove
   B. a woman's rubber shoe
   C. a bone

7. When Henry and Althea leave for church what do Gracie, Zach and Bodie do?
   A. break into the house
   B. dig up the flower bed
   C. look into a cistern

8. Why does Bodie's mother wash him off with a hose?
   A. he fell in a pile of manure
   B. he's covered with wet cement
   C. to calm him down

9. What did Henry Siler bury in his basement?
   A. Perfection, his prize pig
   B. women's clothes
   C. his valuables

10. Where was Bella Siler?
    A. getting her ears tucked
    B. at a fat farm
    C. visiting her mother

MY BUDDY, THE KING
Bill Brittain

1. What is Timothy given for saving a boy from choking?
    A. $100
    B. car
    C. racing bike

2. How does someone try to kill Timothy the night he and Laura eat dinner with Tokab?
    A. run him down
    B. shoot him
    C. poison him

3. What are Ralph, Laura and Timothy given to eat that makes them want to gag?
    A. termites
    B. worms
    C. roaches

4. What game does Tokab say sounds dumb?
    A. bowling
    B. golf
    C. tennis

5. What are Tokab and Timothy doing when the second assassination attempt is made?
    A. eating
    B. sightseeing
    C. playing golf

6. Who is Timothy afraid of?
    A. Arlo Dexter
    B. Fez
    C. Elo

7. How does the president arrive to greet Tokab?
    A. by plane
    B. by limousine
    C. by helicopter

8. Who was the assassin?
    A. Arlo
    B. Elo
    C. Fez

9. Who was the assassin's secret partner?
    A. Arlo Dexter
    B. Elo
    C. Coffin

10. What does Timothy ask Tokab for as a souvenir?
    A. a letter of explanation to his parents
    B. an elephant
    C. a royal ring

MY DANIEL
Pam Conrad

1. Who did Daniel dig a grave for?
   A. his father
   B. his uncle
   C. his baby brother

2. What is Elizabeth always carrying for her grandmother?
   A. shoes
   B. purse
   C. shawl

3. What does Hump Hinton ride?
   A. camel
   B. mule
   C. bison

4. What does Hump Hinton do that startles Julie and her ma?
   A. he starts cursing
   B. he plunges a knife into his thigh
   C. he lets out a war hoop

5. How does Daniel die?
   A. he is shot by Hump Hinton
   B. he drowns in the creek
   C. he is struck by lightning

6. How does Julie get Hump Hinton away from the creek?
   A. she says Amba is ill
   B. she pretends to be hysterical
   C. she holds a gun on him

7. What do Jarvis and Julie do with a small dinosaur bone?
   A. keep it to remember Daniel by
   B. give it to Daniel's parents
   C. put it in Daniel's grave

8. Who killed Hump Hinton?
   A. Jarvis
   B. Amba
   C. Daniel's pa

9. How much did Dr. Crow pay for the dinosaur bones?
   A. $100
   B. $1,000
   C. $50

10. What does Julie give Mr. Crow just before he leaves for the East?
    A. Daniel's fossils and rocks
    B. the dinosaur bone she and Jarvis took
    C. a handshake

MY SISTER IS DRIVING ME CRAZY
Mary E. Ryan

1. What is Pru and Mattie's mom's big announcement?
   A. she applied to NASA
   B. she's having a baby
   C. she's opening a restaurant

2. What does Chloe do?
   A. she's a medium for spirits
   B. she's a school secretary
   C. she's an aerospace engineer

3. What kind of party does Cam have?
   A. hot tub party
   B. ecology party
   C. bird watching party

4. What does Mattie do so she won't look like Pru?
   A. dye her hair purple
   B. cut her hair off
   C. give herself a perm

5. What do Pru and Lydia steal?
   A. the food from a party
   B. Cam's project
   C. Pru's father's mustang

6. Who helps Mattie with her project?
   A. Mattie
   B. Nelson
   C. Cam

7. What kind of contest does Mattie enter?
   A. ecology
   B. science
   C. art

8. What does Mattie put in her project?
   A. swing set
   B. dinosaurs
   C. oil derricks

9. What does the twins' mother like to eat?
   A. health food
   B. donuts
   C. exotic food

10. What does the twins' father do?
    A. teach history
    B. sell beauty supplies
    C. run a golf shop

MY SISTER, MY SCIENCE REPORT
Margaret Bechard

1. Who do Tess and Phoenix want to do their science report on?
   A. Jane
   B. Melissa
   C. Nancy

2. What were Tess and Phoenix supposed to do their science report on?
   A. raccoons
   B. barn owls
   C. bats

3. What is Jane always out of?
   A. shampoo
   B. nail polish
   C. boyfriends

4. How does Jane turn her hair purple?
   A. colored powder
   B. mousse
   C. hair dye

5. Who does Jane like?
   A. Phoenix Guber
   B. Steve Maxwell
   C. Robert Field-Eaton

6. What does Tess win?
   A. ten speed bike
   B. trip to Enchanted Mountain
   C. tickets to Journey to Another Planet

7. Where do Tess and Phoenix follow Jane to?
   A. Valu-Drug
   B. Kroger grocery
   C. Texaco

8. Who turns down the invitation to the ice extravaganza?
   A. Phoenix
   B. Melissa
   C. Jane

9. What does Tess agree to do for Jane so that she help Tess get her prize?
   A. wash the dishes for two weeks
   B. clean out the cat box for a month
   C. iron her clothes for one week

10. How does Guber learn that Tess hates him?
    A. he hears Melissa and Tess at school
    B. he overhears Jane say it
    C. Robert tells him

MY TEACHER GLOWS IN THE DARK
Bruce Coville

1. What does Peter's new name mean?
   A. child of the stars
   B. the wandering one
   C. child without a home

2. What is unusual about Hoo-Lan?
   A. he has eyes on the top of his head
   B. he is blue
   C. he can shrink

3. How does Croc-Doc make Peter better?
   A. he fixes his eye sight
   B. he fixes his hearing
   C. he improves his sense of smell

4. Why is everyone jealous of Peter and humans?
   A. because humans have better mobility
   B. because humans have superior brains
   C. because all humans are different

5. What does Peter have the ability to do that the aliens can't do?
   A. curl his tongue
   B. use intuition
   C. get into people's minds

6. What does Croc-Doc remove from Peter's body?
   A. an alien parasite
   B. a mind control device
   C. his brain

7. Where does Hoo-Lan live on his own planet?
   A. under the sea
   B. on the top of a mountain
   C. in the desert

8. What is the interplanetary council trying to decide?
   A. which planet will rule the earth
   B. whether earth can be part of the interplanetary council
   C. the fate of the earth

9. What is U-RAT?
   A. the name of Hoo-Lan's planet
   B. a device which gives information
   C. the name of the alien ship

10. What happens to everyone every time the ship makes a space-shift?
    A. they faint
    B. they feel like throwing up
    C. their atoms separate

MY TEACHER IS AN ALIEN
Bruce Coville

1. What instrument does Susan play?
   A. bass guitar
   B. oboe
   C. flute

2. What does Peter enjoy doing?
   A. reading
   B. hiking
   C. daydreaming

3. Why does Susan go to Mr. Smith's house?
   A. to get her note back
   B. to discuss her grades
   C. to get a look at his wife

4. What does Mr. Smith not allow Susan's class to do?
   A. go on a field trip
   B. have their annual play
   C. listen to music

5. Where do Susan and Peter find Ms. Schwartz?
   A. closet
   B. basement
   C. attic

6. What happens to time inside a force field?
   A. it stops
   B. it slows down
   C. it speeds up

7. What happens when Susan and Peter put their hands on the force field?
   A. the force field gets stronger
   B. their hands freeze
   C. they can hear Ms. Schwartz' thoughts

8. What does Susan do when she pretends to faint?
   A. look into Mr. Smith's grade book
   B. grab Mr. Smith's ear
   C. look inside Mr. Smith's briefcase

9. What do Stacy and Mike do to keep the alien from choosing them?
   A. stage a fight
   B. become hateful
   C. stop doing homework

10. What hurts the alien?
    A. flute music
    B. bright lights
    C. water

MY UNDERRATED YEAR
Randy Powell

1. What does Mountain do the first day of school?
   A. arrive late
   B. get lost
   C. get suspended

2. What do the Mountains have in their yard?
   A. tennis court
   B. swimming pool
   C. four dogs

3. On what day is the varsity football team chosen?
   A. 66 Day
   B. Labor Day
   C. Alpha Day

4. Where does Roger's mom want to take him?
   A. the school dance
   B. the football banquet
   C. the zoo

5. What happens to Roger when he gets hit hard during the last game of the season?
   A. he throws up
   B. he gets broken ribs
   C. he gets ringing in his ears

6. What does Roger not know how to do?
   A. swim
   B. tie a necktie
   C. fly a kite

7. What football award is Roger given?
   A. most valuable player
   B. hardest hitting
   C. most underrated

8. What does Art give Roger when he takes him into the club locker room?
   A. lecture
   B. beer
   C. hug

9. What do Mary and Roger do on their first date?
   A. go bowling
   B. go skating
   C. go to the movies

10. That evening when the challenge match was over what did Mary Jo do?
    A. buy Roger a coke
    B. cry
    C. celebrate

MYSTERY OF HURRICANE CASTLE
Joan Lowery Nixon

1. Why did Danny get out of the evacuation truck?
    A. he was scared
    B. to find Mrs. Anderson
    C. to get Tobey

2. What did the children find on the table in the castle?
    A. kerosene lamps
    B. candles
    C. flashlights

3. What saved Danny when he slipped off the bluff?
    A. rope around his waist
    B. ledge
    C. tree limb

4. What do Maureen and Kathy find in a long room without furniture?
    A. a museum
    B. beautiful paintings
    C. marble statues

5. What does Maureen do when she panics during the eye of the storm?
    A. run outside
    B. scream
    C. break a window

6. Who does Maureen think the woman in the house might be?
    A. Mrs. Delar
    B. Seaweed Annie
    C. ghost

7. What identifying mark does Mrs. Delar have?
    A. a limp
    B. a crooked nose
    C. a scar on her cheek

8. What is Mrs. Delar afraid of?
    A. thieves
    B. people
    C. snakes

9. What does Mrs. Delar invite the three children to do?
    A. spend next summer with her
    B. have a picnic after the storm is over
    C. sleep with her so they won't be scared

10. After the storm is over who do the children wave to?
    A. the helicopter
    B. the Andersons
    C. Mrs. Delar

MYSTERY OF THE HAUNTED WOODS
Joan Lowery Nixon

1. Who fainted on the stairs?
   A. Neeta
   B. Maureen
   C. Aunt Julia

2. Who does Neeta say haunts the woods?
   A. ghosts of Indian warriors
   B. dead soldiers from the Civil War
   C. her dead husband

3. Why won't Neeta go into the storeroom?
   A. she's afraid of the bear skin rug
   B. it's haunted
   C. she can't go upstairs

4. What do Maureen and Kathy find when they follow the path in the woods?
   A. skeleton
   B. ghost town
   C. wolf

5. What eats out of Lily's hand?
   A. bear
   B. raccoon
   C. deer

6. What keeps disappearing from Aunt Julia's house?
   A. books
   B. food
   C. clothing

7. Who does Kathy sketch?
   A. Neeta
   B. Aunt Julia
   C. Lily

8. Who was Lily sneaking off to meet?
   A. her father
   B. her tutor
   C. her boyfriend

9. What does Aunt Julia give to Danny?
   A. bear rug
   B. teddy bear
   C. an Indian blanket

10. What does Neeta want Lily to do?
    A. find a husband
    B. go to college
    C. get a job

NEXT THING TO STRANGERS
Sheri Cooper Sinykin

1. What is wrong with Jordy?
    A. he's allergic to pollen
    B. he's an alcoholic
    C. he has diabetes

2. Why do Jordy and Cass pass a petition around?
    A. so Cass can stay in the park
    B. so the park will be saved
    C. so they can keep their pets

3. What do Jordy's grandparents do?
    A. call round dances
    B. backpack
    C. referee softball games

4. What does Cass' grandmother like to do?
    A. knit sweaters
    B. play bingo
    C. grow vegetables

5. How do Cass and Jordy meet?
    A. park pool
    B. park street party
    C. while walking their dogs

6. What secret does Cass' grandfather show Jordy?
    A. a stack of bills belonging to Cass' mother
    B. a stack of returned letters
    C. a stack of returned presents

7. What is wrong with Cass' grandmother?
    A. she has bronchitis
    B. she has strepp throat
    C. she needs open heart surgery

8. Who does Jordy call before he and Cass go on their hike?
    A. his mother
    B. the newspapers
    C. his doctor

9. How did Cass' father die?
    A. motorcycle accident
    B. cancer
    C. rodeo accident

10. Why is Jordy in the hospital?
    A. for an insulin problem
    B. he fell off the mountain
    C. he got dehydrated

NIGHT FALL
Joan Aiken

1. What is Meg's father?
   A. doctor
   B. mechanic
   C. writer

2. What is Hodge?
   A. dog
   B. cat
   C. raccoon

3. What is Meg studying to become?
   A. portrait artist
   B. architect
   C. engineer

4. What does Meg's father not allow her to do?
   A. go to school
   B. study in Paris
   C. return to America

5. Who is Meg engaged to?
   A. Toby
   B. Mark
   C. George

6. What does Meg remember in her dream?
   A. running away from a man
   B. being bitten by a dog
   C. falling down a cliff

7. Whose face was in Meg's dreams?
   A. the murdered man's
   B. her father's
   C. Minkins'

8. What does Meg find in her car upon leaving Miss Pentecost?
   A. snake
   B. skunk
   C. rat

9. Who murdered Gerald Trevelyan?
   A. Nab
   B. Mark Trevelyan
   C. Minkins

10. Who rescued Meg and Hodge from the cliff?
    A. Miss Pentecost
    B. Toby
    C. Minkins

NIGHT OF THE WHALE
Jerry Spinelli

1. What do all the kids have in common at school?
   A. they all work on the school paper
   B. they are all in honors classes
   C. they are all on the student council

2. What is Lauren doing in the picture Digger takes of her?
   A. taking out the trash
   B. picking her nose
   C. posing like a model

3. What does Mouse see on Lauren that shocks him?
   A. black hair on her chest
   B. pink shortie nightgown
   C. tatoo of an anchor

4. What does Mouse buy at the store?
   A. men's cologne
   B. colored underwear
   C. neon swim trunks

5. What disgusting thing does Digger do when people are eating?
   A. pick his nose
   B. talk about the food
   C. fart

6. What kind of whales were beached?
   A. killer
   B. sperm
   C. pilot

7. Who loses her boyfriend to a lady midshipman?
   A. Lauren
   B. Timmi
   C. Wags

8. Who is in a wheelchair?
   A. Lauren
   B. Timmi
   C. Wags

9. How many whales were stranded?
   A. 9
   B. 29
   C. 54

10. Why doesn't Digger return home at the end of the week?
    A. he wants to hitchhike across America
    B. he wants to take care of a baby whale
    C. he's going to marry Tennessee

THE NIGHT THE WHITE DEER DIED
Gary Paulsen

1. What does Janet's mother sell at the festival?
   A. stone sculptures
   B. nachos
   C. Indian jewelry

2. Who cleans the grounds after the festival?
   A. park rangers
   B. drunks from the jail
   C. merchants

3. What does Janet ask Julio to do?
   A. pose for her mother
   B. walk her home
   C. teach her to ride a horse

4. Where does Billy take Janet?
   A. to Mexico
   B. to his pueblo
   C. to church

5. What does Billy leave on Janet's doorstep?
   A. letter
   B. spear
   C. kachina doll

6. Who follows Janet home?
   A. a drunk
   B. Julio
   C. stray dog

7. What does Janet like?
   A. to be alone
   B. to swim
   C. to collect rocks

8. What does Billy do outside Janet's window at night?
   A. throw rocks
   B. whistle
   C. play a flute

9. What does the horse Billy brings do when it hears the flute?
   A. bucks
   B. dances
   C. neighs

10. What is on the pony?
    A. saddle
    B. painted pictures
    C. bells

THE NIGHT THE WHOLE CLASS SLEPT OVER
Stella Pevsner

1. What does BJ say she has given to the class?
   A. encouragement
   B. the curse
   C. the pox

2. What does Felix have three of at his house?
   A. computers
   B. dogs
   C. bathrooms

3. Who does no one at school like?
   A. BJ
   B. Felix
   C. Amanda

4. What does Dan help Amanda build?
   A. doghouse
   B. snow woman
   C. science project

5. Why does the principal dismiss school early?
   A. for a teacher's meeting
   B. for Christmas vacation
   C. for a snowball fight

6. What is unusual about Martha?
   A. she can read
   B. she doesn't talk
   C. she can play chess

7. Who is BJ related to?
   A. Martha
   B. Amanda
   C. Felix

8. How do BJ and Felix get the doctor?
   A. smoke signals
   B. skate across the lake
   C. ham radio

9. Who becomes sick at the sleep over?
   A. Martha
   B. Dan
   C. Amanda

10. What do Dan's classmates say he is?
    A. artist
    B. moron
    C. nerd

NO DRAGONS TO SLAY
Jan Greenberg

1. Who does Thomas' father get him a blind date with?
   A. a girl in a back brace
   B. a blind girl
   C. a college student

2. What does Thomas collect?
   A. marbles
   B. flint stones and arrowheads
   C. model cars and planes

3. What medicine does the doctor give Thomas?
   A. marijuana capsules
   B. Valium
   C. Tylenol IV

4. What does Thomas' father want him to do when he loses his hair?
   A. wear a cap
   B. wear a wig
   C. go bald

5. What does everyone keep asking Thomas?
   A. How do you feel?
   B. What is it like to have cancer?
   C. Are you seeing any of your friends?

6. Where does Thomas find Nicky when he runs away at school?
   A. in the restroom
   B. at McDonald's
   C. in a tree

7. Where does Thomas invite Ana to go?
   A. art museum
   B. school play
   C. soccer game

8. Where does Thomas live while at the dig?
   A. tent
   B. motel
   C. priest's house

9. Who was hurt at the dig site?
   A. Penny
   B. Milton
   C. Thomas

10. What does Thomas help Nicky do?
    A. learn to read
    B. plant pumpkin seeds
    C. learn to spit

NOTHING BUT THE TRUTH
Avi

1. What does Miss Narwin want money from the district for?
   A. to buy textbooks
   B. for a field trip
   C. to take a professional class

2. What sport is Philip good at?
   A. track
   B. soccer
   C. baseball

3. How many days does Miss Narwin ask Philip to stop singing in homeroom?
   A. 3
   B. 4
   C. 6

4. What does the vice-principal ask Philip to do in place of being suspended?
   A. take lunch detention
   B. apologize
   C. write a 300 word paper on following the rules

5. How do most of the students feel about Miss Narwin?
   A. they hate her
   B. they are indifferent to her
   C. they like her

6. Why do the school administrators say Philip was suspended?
   A. for singing
   B. for being disrespectful
   C. for encouraging others to disobey the rules

7. What subject is Philip almost failing?
   A. math
   B. science
   C. English

8. What does Philip ask Miss Narwin for?
   A. an apology
   B. extra work
   C. a second chance to behave

9. What happened to Miss Narwin?
   A. she took the rest of the year off
   B. she committed suicide
   C. she continued to teach

10. Why does Philip start crying when asked to lead the class in singing the Star Spangled Banner at his new school?
    A. he doesn't know the words
    B. he was afraid the teacher was making fun of him
    C. he hates the song now

ONE FAT SUMMER
Robert Lipstyle

1. What does Bobby's father want him to do for the summer?
   A. take it easy
   B. get a job
   C. go to camp

2. What does Dr. Kahn do at the end of Bobby's second day of work?
   A. lower his pay
   B. give him a raise
   C. fire him

3. What does Bobby buy with his first day's pay?
   A. new lawn mower blade
   B. lunch at a sit down restaurant
   C. large nice pants

4. What did Willie do to Bobby on the island?
   A. beat him up
   B. strip him
   C. tie him up

5. Who rescued Bobby from the island?
   A. Pete Marino
   B. Dr. Kahn
   C. Jim Smith

6. What kind of operation did Joanie have?
   A. toes straightened
   B. nose job
   C. plastic surgery to remove a scar

7. What does Bobby not do for Dr. Kahn?
   A. clean out the gutter
   B. mop the pool deck
   C. paint his fence

8. Who does Michelle like?
   A. Jim Smith
   B. Pete Marino
   C. Willie Rumson

9. What do Bobby's parents argue about?
   A. his mother getting a job
   B. paying for Michelle's college
   C. buying a new car

10. What does Bobby do to Willie?
    A. hold him under water
    B. beat him up
    C. turn him into the police

ONE-EYED CAT
Paula Fox

1. Who is Mrs. Scallop?
   A. housekeeper
   B. gardener
   C. pharmacist

2. Why is Ned's mother in a wheelchair?
   A. she broke her leg
   B. she has rheumatic arthritis
   C. she is paralyzed

3. Who gave Ned the rifle?
   A. Uncle Hilary
   B. Mrs. Scallop
   C. Mr. Scully

4. What does Ned not want to do?
   A. babysit for Mrs. Kimball
   B. go on vacation with Uncle Hilary
   C. see the cat

5. What happened to Mr. Scully?
   A. he fell down the stairs
   B. he froze in the snow
   C. he had a stroke

6. Outside of who's house does the cat get food?
   A. Mrs. Kimball's
   B. Ned's
   C. Mr. Scully's

7. Who does Ned tell first about shooting the cat?
   A. Mr. Scully
   B. his mother
   C. Mrs. Scallop

8. What does Ned's father do?
   A. he's a farmer
   B. he's a barber
   C. he's a minister

9. Who saw Ned from the attic window the night he shot the cat?
   A. his father
   B. his mother
   C. Mrs. Scallop

10. Who does Ned walk home from the Makepeace house in the middle of the night with?
    A. Mr. Scully
    B. his mother
    C. Mrs. Scallop

THE OVERNIGHT

R.L. Stine

1. What is Della doing when she gets lost in the woods?
   A. blazing a trail
   B. hunting for firewood
   C. playing war games

2. How does Della kill the strange man?
   A. she shoves him over the ravine
   B. she hits him with her flashlight
   C. she shoots him with his gun

3. What does Ricky spend most of his time doing?
   A. telling jokes
   B. flexing his muscles
   C. eating

4. What does Della find is missing when she returns from the island?
   A. her school ID
   B. her wallet
   C. her flashlight

5. Who gets skulls sent to them in envelopes?
   A. Pete and Suki
   B. Ricky and Maia
   C. Gary and Della

6. What does Gary do when the dead man's partner knocks on Della's door?
   A. scream
   B. take a picture
   C. tackle him

7. What happens on Pete and Della's first date?
   A. Pete's tires are slashed
   B. they find a message on Pete's car
   C. they are in a car chase

8. Why does the group return for a second overnight?
   A. to bury the body
   B. to get Della's zap gun
   C. to overcome their fears

9. Who is hit over the head on the second overnight?
   A. Mr. Abner
   B. Maia
   C. Pete

10. Who saves Della from the dead man?
    A. Pete
    B. Gary
    C. Ricky

OVERNIGHT SENSATION
Joan Lowery Nixon

1. What does Cassie think about the people at her mother's parties?
   A. they're smart and funny
   B. they're people she should know
   C. they're shallow and superficial

2. Where does Abby go for two weeks that Cassie does not approve of?
   A. Vietnam
   B. on a trip with Arthur
   C. to see Cassie's father

3. What does Cassie not tell Marc about herself at first?
   A. that she is Abby Grant's daughter
   B. that she is younger than he is
   C. that she is divorced

4. What did Abby not show up for?
   A. Cassie's high school graduation
   B. opening night of the senior class play
   C. her own party

5. Who is Arthur?
   A. Abby's agent
   B. Abby's husband
   C. Abby's boyfriend

6. Who is always asking Abby for money?
   A. Cassie
   B. Bobby
   C. Arthur

7. How does Cassie raise money for Marc's film?
   A. singing and dancing
   B. becoming a prostitute
   C. selling her photo layout

8. What do Cassie and Abby do on the Jackie Gleason special?
   A. tell jokes
   B. a skit with a fight
   C. sing together

9. Who arranges for Cassie to get a setting with a portfolio photographer?
   A. Bobby
   B. her agent, Al
   C. Abby

10. How does Cassie help with Bobby's film?
    A. as an actress
    B. as an assistant director
    C. with the costume design

THE PARTY'S OVER
Caroline B. Cooney

1. What does Jaz tap out morse code on?
   A. desk
   B. loud speaker
   C. car horn

2. Who delivered pizza to the graduation rehearsal?
   A. gorilla
   B. clown
   C. big bird

3. What kind of diet is Meg on?
   A. swear
   B. food
   C. shopping

4. What was in the small box Jaz gave Hallie?
   A. diamond ring
   B. roll of stamps
   C. quarter for the phone

5. Who does Hallie visit on campus?
   A. Jaz
   B. Gretchen
   C. Flavia

6. What job does Hallie get that she likes?
   A. waitress at the Sea Scape
   B. office work at the marina
   C. wire work at the factory

7. When does Jaz break up with Hallie?
   A. prom night
   B. spring break
   C. Thanksgiving weekend

8. What does Hallie buy with the money from her job?
   A. small boat
   B. truck
   C. car

9. Who kisses Hallie on New Year's?
   A. Johnny
   B. Timmie
   C. Royce

10. How do Hallie's friends describe her?
    A. bossy
    B. good listener
    C. lazy

THE PIGMAN
Paul Zindel

...ine contact Mr. Pignati in the beginning?

... Pignati collect?
A. ...
B. butterflies
C. rocks

3. Where do John, Lorraine and the Pigman go?
   A. zoo
   B. museum
   C. farm

4. What is Bobo?
   A. dog
   B. baboon
   C. clown

5. What does Lorraine's mother do for a living?
   A. caterer
   B. truck driver
   C. private nurse

6. Where does Mr. Pignati say his wife is?
   A. in the hospital
   B. in California
   C. visiting her mother

7. What does Mr. Pignati buy for John and Lorraine?
   A. jackets
   B. walkmans
   C. roller skates

8. Why was Mr. Pignati in the hospital?
   A. stomach cramps
   B. heart attack
   C. concussion

9. What do John and Lorraine do while Mr. Pignati is in the hospital?
   A. have a party
   B. go to church
   C. go camping

10. Who slapped Lorraine?
    A. her mother
    B. Mr. Pignati
    C. John

162

THE PIGMAN'S LEGACY
Paul Zindel

1. What do John and Lorraine bring to the old man?
    A. space heater
    B. blankets
    C. marble pecan fudge

2. Where does the old man accuse John and Lorraine of being from?
    A. IRS
    B. the nursing home
    C. the funeral home

3. What is the only game the old man knows?
    A. the game of life
    B. croquet
    C. checkers

4. What has the old man always liked to do?
    A. write poetry
    B. dig
    C. tend flower gardens

5. What does Gus want John and Lorraine to help him get from the Colonel's house?
    A. his maps
    B. his tools
    C. his truck

6. Why did John and Lorraine take the Colonel to the hospital?
    A. fainting spells
    B. stomach cramps
    C. concussion

7. What did the Colonel do for a living?
    A. manage an amusement park
    B. find oil
    C. design subways

8. What do Dolly, the Colonel, John and Lorraine do in Atlantic City?
    A. visit the Colonel's children
    B. gamble
    C. see Stone Mountain

9. What does the Colonel ask for while in the hospital?
    A. a priest
    B. some fudge
    C. his wife

10. What do John and Lorraine bring into the hospital?
    A. German shepherd
    B. Lorraine's mother
    C. marble pecan fudge

PILLOW OF CLOUDS
Marc Talbert

1. What is the surprise Chester's mother has for him when he returns home?
   A. redecorated room
   B. season tickets to the Baltimore Oreoles
   C. built in swimming pool

2. What does Chester's mother want to buy him?
   A. computer
   B. car
   C. stereo

3. What does Chester return to his mother's home to get?
   A. his stash of poems
   B. his guitar
   C. his dog

4. What do Jose and Chester see burned up during Fiesta?
   A. picture
   B. statue
   C. house

5. What is Chester's mother's problem?
   A. she's a hooker
   B. she's a thief
   C. she's an alcoholic

6. What possession is Arturo proud of?
   A. his jewelry
   B. low rider car
   C. an autographed football

7. What is Jose good at?
   A. telling stories
   B. soccer
   C. drawing

8. What do Chester's father and Florence do during Fiesta?
   A. run a food stand
   B. get married
   C. tell the history of fiesta to tourists

9. What was the bad news about Chester's mother?
   A. she tried to kill herself
   B. she was mugged
   C. she was in a car accident

10. What is Chester's father's new project?
    A. to write a novel
    B. to build a car
    C. to build a room onto his house

THE PLACE OF LIONS
Eric Campbell

1. What causes the plane to crash?
   A. a bomb
   B. a fuel leak
   C. birds

2. What was Mike shooting at?
   A. poachers
   B. elephants
   C. tigers

3. Who is Henry?
   A. the custodian
   B. the mechanic
   C. the principal

4. Why were Mike and his father moving to Africa?
   A. to go to college
   B. for an engineering job
   C. to experience wildlife

5. What did Chris use to make the shelter for his father?
   A. metal
   B. trees
   C. sheets

6. What was wrong with Chris' father?
   A. broken jaw
   B. broken leg
   C. bloody chest wound

7. Why was the lion traveling alone and not with the pride?
   A. he preferred to hunt alone
   B. he was seeking a lioness
   C. he was going home to die

8. What were the poachers trying to kill?
   A. leopards
   B. elephants
   C. zebras

9. What happened a year after the crash?
   A. rescuers and crash victims met on the hill
   B. Mike and his father moved back to America
   C. Chris was killed by a lion

10. Why were the poachers chasing Chris?
    A. to kidnap him
    B. to rescue him
    C. to kill him

A PLACE TO BELONG

Joan Lowery Nixon

1. What happens to Danny the first day of school?
   A. he fights Wilmer
   B. he forgets his lunch
   C. he has to stand in the corner

2. What does Danny lose?
   A. his money
   B. the addresses of his family
   C. his homework

3. What was Dr. Mundy trying to pass off as medicine?
   A. old river water
   B. liquor
   C. cherry flavored water

4. What are all the kids at school fighting over?
   A. the score on a baseball game
   B. the issue of slavery
   C. insulting a family

5. Why was the Christmas pageant cancelled?
   A. lack of participation
   B. bad weather
   C. fighting

6. What is Melba given?
   A. hair ribbon
   B. kitten
   C. old dress

7. Who does Melba want Alfrid to marry?
   A. Ennie Pratka
   B. Noreen Kelly
   C. Katherine Banks

8. Who does Noreen Kelly marry?
   A. Alfrid
   B. Mundy
   C. John Murphy

9. How was Danny able to capture the Southern sympathizers who attacked the farm?
   A. by smoking them out
   B. by tripping their horses with twine
   C. by surrounding them

10. After Noreen marries, which of her children live with her?
    A. Danny
    B. Peg
    C. Frankie

POPCORN DAYS AND BUTTERMILK NIGHTS
Gary Paulsen

1. What does Uncle David do for a living?
   A. blacksmith
   B. rancher
   C. store owner

2. What does Uncle David's family use for chairs at storytime?
   A. crates
   B. logs
   C. benches

3. What does David's family not have?
   A. money
   B. friends
   C. good health

4. What does Carley do after being dragged by a calf?
   A. run away
   B. hit Tinker
   C. laugh

5. What nationality is David?
   A. Irish
   B. English
   C. Norwegian

6. What does the town of Norsten not have?
   A. sheriff
   B. doctor
   C. electricity

7. What does David build for the town?
   A. circus
   B. church
   C. hangman's gallows

8. What did David do in Minneapolis that got him in trouble?
   A. steal a purse
   B. steal a horse
   C. burn down a garage

9. How many people share a bedroom with Carley?
   A. 0
   B. 7
   C. 15

10. Why does Jenny's dad send for Carley?
    A. to help him load their wagon
    B. to help take Uncle David home
    C. to get him to find the sheriff

PRAIRIE SONGS
Pam Conrad

1. What does Clara do in exchange for Emmeline teaching her children reading, writing and math?
   A. her gardening
   B. her cooking
   C. her laundry

2. What is broken that causes Emmeline to become hysterical?
   A. crib
   B. crystal bowl
   C. china doll

3. What does Clara use for fuel in her stove?
   A. cow chips
   B. wood
   C. coal

4. Why is Clara worried about Lester?
   A. he is lazy
   B. he doesn't talk much
   C. he is a bully

5. Why does Doc threaten to kill Paulie if he ever sees him again?
   A. he stole from Emmeline
   B. he threw a dead snake on Emmeline
   C. he tried to shoot his own mother

6. Why does Louisa think Emmeline is dead?
   A. she saw Lester shoot at her
   B. she fell and water poured out of her
   C. she saw buzzards circling where Emmeline fell

7. What terrible tragedy happens that causes the Doc and the men to leave for a few days?
   A. Indians attacked a settlement
   B. a prairie fire
   C. a train wreck

8. What happened to Cap, Louisa's family's horse?
   A. he ran away
   B. Indians stole him
   C. he died

9. How does Emmeline die?
   A. she froze to death outside
   B. she was killed by Indians
   C. she starved to death

10. What do Clara, Lester and Louisa see at the 4th of July celebration?
    A. photos of settlers
    B. a horse race
    C. a wresting match

PROFESSOR POPKIN'S PRODIGIOUS POLISH
Bill Brittain

1. Who does Luther's mother say he has to take with him on his 3 days off?
   A. Bertram
   B. Simon
   C. Dorcas

2. What does Luther polish at his own house?
   A. toy soldiers and an awl
   B. silverware
   C. kitchen table

3. What does Bertram do with his toy soldiers?
   A. burns them in the stove
   B. buries them
   C. throws them in the pond

4. Who does Luther go on a ride with in the middle of the night?
   A. Stew Meat
   B. Professor Mordecai Popkin
   C. Elias Obern

5. Who warns Luther that something is not right about the letter?
   A. Hazel Quist
   B. Bertram
   C. Stew Meat

6. What does Bertram use the polish on?
   A. fiddle and pipe
   B. school bell and buzz saw
   C. printing press

7. What do Dorcas and Hester have put in the fire station's pumper wagon?
   A. water
   B. small rocks
   C. lye soap

8. What did Luther do with the rest of the polish?
   A. keep it
   B. send it back
   C. destroy it

9. Who likes Luther?
   A. Dorcas
   B. Hester
   C. Hazel

10. What keeps charging at Luther like a bull?
    A. saw table
    B. stove
    C. wooden doll

PROM DRESS
Lael Littke

1. What does Robin get a scholarship for?
   A. dancing
   B. grades
   C. sports

2. What happens to Robin when she wears the dress?
   A. she is killed
   B. her feet are crushed
   C. she is in a car wreck

3. What does Felicia do for a living?
   A. nurse
   B. zoo keeper
   C. program computers

4. What does Felicia lose when she wears the dress?
   A. her wealth
   B. her self respect
   C. her job

5. Where does Nicole find the dress?
   A. in a store
   B. in the trash
   C. on the bus

6. What happens to Nicole when she wears the dress?
   A. she is mauled by a dog
   B. she goes crazy
   C. she gets amnesia

7. What does Gabriette like to do most?
   A. play the piano
   B. watch old movies
   C. read books

8. What happens to Miss Catherine when she wears the dress?
   A. she falls down a well
   B. she loses an arm
   C. her face is burned with acid

9. Why does Rowena want the girls to wear the dress and get hurt?
   A. because they're wealthy
   B. because they're beautiful and have boyfriends
   C. because they're smart and young

10. What does Felicia want to do with the dress?
    A. throw it away
    B. destroy it
    C. keep it forever

THE RAIN CATCHERS

Jean Thesman

1. Who is dying?
   A. Yolanda
   B. Olivia
   C. Belle

2. What does Colleen sell at the flea market that belongs to Fawn?
   A. raspberry teddy
   B. gold bracelet
   C. sequin purse

3. What does Belle do that upsets Gray?
   A. she gets Aaron to take Gray out
   B. she quits her job at the hospital
   C. she stops speaking to Yolanda

4. What does Aaron do all summer?
   A. train his dog, Gip
   B. paint Gray's home
   C. work at the hardware store

5. Who moves into Gray's home?
   A. Aaron
   B. Dancer
   C. Colleen

6. What does Gray tell Dancer she wants to buy?
   A. stereo
   B. gun
   C. gold chain

7. Who beats up Colleen?
   A. Fawn
   B. Dr. Clement
   C. Lance

8. What does Dr. Clement accuse Belle of?
   A. spreading lies about him
   B. killing Olivia
   C. corrupting Gray

9. Who gets married?
   A. Belle
   B. Yolanda
   C. Colleen

10. What do the women of the house do every afternoon?
    A. have tea
    B. take a nap
    C. go shopping

RANDALL'S WALL
Carol Fenner

1. What does Randall name the deer he drew?
   A. Butterfly
   B. Heart
   C. Singapore

2. Why did Randall's teacher throw away the drawing of his mother?
   A. she said it was a dirty picture
   B. he drew it during math
   C. it was being passed around the class

3. What does Randall's house not have?
   A. water
   B. heat
   C. electricity

4. Who has a black eye?
   A. Georgie
   B. Jean
   C. Randall

5. What is unusual about the way Jean dresses?
   A. she wears army boots
   B. she wears a bullet belt
   C. she wears paper clip jewelry

6. What floats to the surface during Randall's bath?
   A. pink ball of play doe
   B. part of a cheeseburger
   C. pencil stub

7. What did Randall do when he found his notebook missing?
   A. cry
   B. scream
   C. faint

8. Who does Randall write a letter to?
   A. his teacher
   B. his uncle
   C. his father

9. How does Randall get to school on parent's day?
   A. he walks
   B. he takes the bus
   C. he rides with his mother

10. What are the spots on Randall's arms from?
    A. bed bugs
    B. cigarette burns
    C. ring worms

RED CAP
G. Clifton Wisler

1. What does R.J. do when he first joins the infantry and they make fun of his size?
   A. he runs away
   B. he sets out to capture the enemy alone
   C. he puts too much pepper in the stew

2. Why are both the Rebs and the Yanks angry with Grant?
   A. he stopped the prisoner exchange
   B. for dragging out the war
   C. for cruelty to prisoners

3. What is a 'shebang'?
   A. a makeshift tent
   B. a loud party
   C. a secret weapon

4. In Andersonville what do the Yanks give to the Rebs in exchange for food?
   A. information
   B. brass Union buttons
   C. do their laundry

5. What do many of the prisoners at Andersonville prison die of?
   A. small pox
   B. dysentery
   C. scurvy

6. What does Red Cap do for Captain Wirz?
   A. laundry
   B. accounts
   C. errands

7. What does Captain Wirz accuse Red Cap of doing?
   A. stealing food
   B. spying
   C. making escape maps

8. What did the Yanks in Andersonville do to six of the New York raiders?
   A. shoot them
   B. hang them
   C. beat them to death

9. How many men of the Company 'I' 10th West Virginia Volunteer Infantry left Andersonville prison alive?
   A. one
   B. three
   C. five

10. What did R.J. Powell say he was in order to leave Andersonville prison in a prisoner exchange?
    A. a sailor
    B. a calvary soldier
    C. an infantry soldier

THE REVOLVING DOOR STOPS HERE
Phyllis Anderson Wood

1. What medical problem does Eric have?
    A. diabetic
    B. epilepsy
    C. asthma

2. Why is Eric taken away from his fourth foster home?
    A. the wife is an alcoholic
    B. the wife died
    C. the wife is an abuser

3. Why does Eric have to leave Faye's home?
    A. her daughter's family is moving in
    B. Faye does not like Eric
    C. Faye is too old to keep him

4. Where does Eric's father live?
    A. Mexico
    B. Alaska
    C. India

5. Why is Susan in the hospital?
    A. she's having knee surgery
    B. she's getting a cyst removed
    C. she's having a baby

6. Who is Eric's caseworker?
    A. Amy
    B. Lorna
    C. Olive

7. What is Cleo?
    A. dog
    B. guitar
    C. truck

8. What does Amy teach Eric how to do?
    A. bait a hook
    B. race leaves over the dam
    C. catch tadpoles

9. What does Eric's father give him?
    A. stock in an oil company
    B. an engraved watch
    C. a mountain bike

10. What are Eric and Roger going to build?
    A. a garage apartment
    B. a deck
    C. a bird house

THE RIVER
Gary Paulsen

1. What does Brian call the 54 days he was in the wilderness?
   A. The Time
   B. The Ordeal
   C. The Trial

2. What does Brian love to do now that he didn't before he was in the woods?
   A. take baths
   B. cook
   C. sleep outside

3. What does Derek tell Brian to do?
   A. externalize
   B. leave the gear behind
   C. take the food with them

4. Where is Brian trying to take Derek?
   A. ranger station
   B. trading post
   C. local campground

5. What terrible thought came into Brian's mind while they were on the river?
   A. they were going to die
   B. the raft would break
   C. to get rid of Derek

6. What causes Brian to fall off the raft?
   A. a waterfall
   B. taking a bend in the river too fast
   C. hitting a submerged boulder

7. What does Derek give to Brian?
   A. a canoe with paddles
   B. an award
   C. invitation to teach survival skills as a career

8. What can't Brian figure out?
   A. how to get the logs to the river
   B. how to get Derek to stay on the raft
   C. how to get Derek to drink without choking

9. What does Brian pull the raft to shore to do?
   A. go to the restroom
   B. make a canopy for Derek
   C. sleep

10. Where does Brian get the logs to make the raft?
    A. drift wood from the store
    B. logs the beavers have cut
    C. trees he has cut himself

ROBO DAD
Alden R. Carter

1. What was Shar's dad doing when his artery burst?
    A. driving a forklift
    B. climbing stairs
    C. fishing

2. What part of Shar's dad's brain was affected by the burst artery?
    A. coordination
    B. emotions
    C. speech

3. Why does Shar's Dad throw his food and glass at the picnic?
    A. his sons stopped playing catch with him
    B. he doesn't like the food
    C. no one is listening to him

4. Who almost drowns while skiing?
    A. Shar
    B. Sid
    C. Bob Marsten

5. What does Shar's mother do?
    A. sell vacuum cleaners
    B. sell Avon
    C. sell real estate

6. What does Paul like to build?
    A. clay villages
    B. sugar cube igloos
    C. toothpick bridges

7. What does Shar accuse her mother of?
    A. having an affair
    B. getting a divorce
    C. not telling her the truth

8. What does Shar give to Bob Marsten?
    A. car keys
    B. boat
    C. shotgun shells

9. Why are Shar's Dad's hunting friends concerned about him?
    A. he almost shot one of them
    B. he shot three times the limit
    C. he is shooting the wrong animals

10. What is Shar's mom afraid her husband will do?
    A. get lost
    B. commit suicide
    C. hurt the kids

A ROYAL PAIN
Ellen Conford

1. Who does Abby fall in love with?
   A. baker
   B. bartender
   C. journalist

2. What question does Abby ask that no one will answer?
   A. when the wedding is to take place
   B. what Casimir is like
   C. when she will become the ruler

3. What does Prince Casimir do to embarrass Abby at the engagement ball?
   A. he makes her skirt go up
   B. he trips her
   C. he spills punch on her

4. What does the prince give to Abby?
   A. monkey
   B. dog
   C. horse

5. How does Abby fake her suicide?
   A. she pretends to have taken sleeping pills
   B. she pretends to have taken poison
   C. she pretends to jump out of a window

6. Who does Dolores always talk to?
   A. Mickey Mouse
   B. Snoopy
   C. Casper the Ghost

7. How does Abby try to anger the princess?
   A. by giving away some of the crown jewels
   B. by inviting commoners to stay in the castle
   C. by roller skating in the castle

8. What does Abby get her picture made for?
   A. statue
   B. stamp
   C. coin

9. What does Abby do to try to get Prince Casimir to not like her?
   A. she dresses like a punk
   B. she is extremely rude to him
   C. she pretends to be an air head

10. What does Geoffrey do to save Abby from marrying Casimir?
    A. exposes Abby as a fake
    B. proves her to be insane
    C. prints a scandalous story

RUMBLE FISH

S.E. Hinton

1. Who is Rusty-James' best friend?
   A. Benny
   B. Smokey
   C. Steve

2. Why was Motorcycle Boy expelled?
   A. having perfect semester tests
   B. fighting
   C. cursing out a teacher

3. What is Rusty-James scared of?
   A. being alone
   B. being shot
   C. not being accepted into a gang

4. What did Motorcycle Boy do when Rusty-James was cut?
   A. take him to the hospital
   B. pour wine on the cut
   C. sew him up

5. What does Motorcycle Boy hate?
   A. violence
   B. his mother
   C. drugs

6. What was Rusty-James attempting to steal?
   A. car
   B. hubcaps
   C. gun

7. Who does Motorcycle Boy see in California?
   A. his girl
   B. a drug dealer
   C. his mother

8. Who beat up Steve?
   A. Rusty-James
   B. his dad
   C. B.J. and Smokey

9. What does Motorcycle Boy do when he breaks into the pet store?
   A. set the animals free
   B. take a puppy
   C. steal the money

10. Who was out to get Motorcycle Boy?
    A. Patterson
    B. Steve
    C. Marty

RUN
William Sleator

1. What is missing from Lillian's house?
   A. jewelry
   B. stereo
   C. radio

2. What happens to Lillian at dinner?
   A. she gets drunk
   B. she falls out of her chair
   C. she throws up

3. Why do Mark and Jerry stay with Lillian on the first day?
   A. because it is raining
   B. because Mark likes her
   C. because they want to case the joint

4. What is Mark interested in?
   A. soccer
   B. the herring run
   C. fishing

5. How does Lillian meet Mark and Jerry?
   A. they ran into each other at the grocery store
   B. her parents introduced them
   C. by rescuing them

6. Who doesn't want to call the police?
   A. Jerry
   B. Mark
   C. Lillian

7. Where is Lillian when she talks to the strange man alone?
   A. in the woods
   B. in the living room
   C. in bed

8. What does Mark break?
   A. mirror
   B. lantern
   C. leg

9. Who gets shot?
   A. the man
   B. Mark
   C. Jerry

10. What are Lillian's parents really picky about?
    A. having a spotless house
    B. personal safety
    C. being educated

RUSTY FERTLANDER, LADY'S MAN
Christi Killien

1. What is Rusty's father?
   A. minister
   B. farmer
   C. electrician

2. How does Rusty do when he wrestles Susan?
   A. he wins
   B. he loses
   C. he ties

3. Why does Rusty wrestle Susan?
   A. to impress Dayna
   B. the coach makes him
   C. his parents make him

4. What is the name of the comic hero Rusty invented when he was younger?
   A. Galaxy Master
   B. Molar Maximillian
   C. Larry Luster

5. Who is Hymnal?
   A. Rusty's music teacher
   B. the school mascot
   C. the family dog

6. What cartoon villain does Rusty create for the school paper?
   A. Sweaty Socks and Son of Sweaty Socks
   B. Bobby Bully and Son of Bobby Bully
   C. Jammed Locker and Son of Jammed Locker

7. What does Rusty's hero for the school cartoon look like?
   A. an ordinary guy
   B. a jock
   C. a nerd

8. What does Rusty do to make himself feel more macho?
   A. change his walk
   B. change his talk
   C. change his haircut

9. Who does Rusty practice his wrestling moves on at home?
   A. his sister
   B. stuffed gorilla
   C. large pillow

10. What causes Rusty to break out in a rash?
    A. nerves
    B. Magna soap
    C. bee sting

SATURNALIA
Paul Fleischman

1. What does Malcolm give to several girls he likes?
    A. candy
    B. grapes
    C. oranges

2. Who does Mr. Speke grieve for?
    A. his dead daughter
    B. his dead wife
    C. his dead son

3. Who does William find through his flute playing?
    A. his cousin and father's uncle
    B. his brother
    C. his grandmother and sister

4. What kind of Indian is William?
    A. Shawnee
    B. Nagarranset
    C. Chippawah

5. Why does Mr. Speke take the Indian girl, Ninnomi home?
    A. to marry her
    B. to serve him
    C. to sketch her

6. During Saturnalia what does Gwenne find inside her custard?
    A. gold coin
    B. miniature crown
    C. silver ring

7. What does Malcolm suggest the wigmaker do just before Madam Phipp's dinner?
    A. propose to her on his knees
    B. kidnap her
    C. climb through her chamber window

8. What was in the silver sugar bowl Mr. Hogwood gave to Madam Phipp?
    A. wedding ring
    B. severed mouse head
    C. sugar

9. Who was murdered with an awl?
    A. Mr. Rudd
    B. Mr. Baggot
    C. Mr. Trulliber

10. What does William's uncle suggest William do after the murder?
    A. run away with them
    B. confess
    C. get married

SAY GOODNIGHT, GRACIE
Julie Reece Deaver

1. What does Jimmy want to be?
   A. professional dancer
   B. football player
   C. astronaut

2. What is Morgan afraid of?
   A. spiders
   B. needles
   C. high places

3. Where does Morgan's aunt work?
   A. hospital
   B. morgue
   C. print shop

4. What happens to Morgan on stage the first time she's in a real play?
   A. she does great
   B. she trips and falls on her face
   C. she knocks over the scenery

5. What does Morgan wear to bed?
   A. a long flannel gown
   B. Jimmy's scarf
   C. Jimmy's jacket

6. What does Morgan do with the sleeping pills?
   A. takes them all
   B. sells them
   C. throws them into the river

7. What does Jimmy's mother give Morgan for her eighteenth birthday?
   A. Jimmy's gold baby ring
   B. flowers
   C. Jimmy's photo album

8. What do Jimmy's parents do to celebrate Jimmy's eighteenth birthday?
   A. have a party
   B. show old home movies of Jimmy
   C. establish a scholarship fund

9. What news does Jimmy's mother give to Morgan when Morgan visits?
   A. she is seeing a counselor
   B. she is going to have a baby
   C. they are moving away

10. What does Morgan finally do with Jimmy's jacket?
    A. throw it away
    B. throw it in the river
    C. pack it up and store it

SCARED STIFF
Willo Davis Roberts

1. Where does Uncle Henry live?
   A. in a camper
   B. in a green box car
   C. in a purple bus

2. What does Rick think the men who ransacked his apartment were looking for?
   A. papers
   B. murder weapon
   C. money

3. Where do Rick's parents work?
   A. E & F Trucking
   B. Accounting Inc.
   C. Movers Limited

4. What does Rick fall through?
   A. floor of the fun house
   B. shed roof
   C. roller coaster track

5. Why was Rick's dad in trouble with his boss?
   A. he knew too much
   B. he was caught embezzling
   C. his load was hijacked

6. What do the kidnappers drive?
   A. pink jeep
   B. black sedan
   C. red sports car

7. Where does Rick think Sophie called him from?
   A. the town dump
   B. the Dairy Queen
   C. the dog pound

8. Who helped Kenny and Rick escape from the kidnappers?
   A. Cranston and Julie
   B. Julie and Connie
   C. Connie and Zimmer

9. How does Rick fool Zimmer in the cave?
   A. by sinking his own gondola
   B. by swimming under Zimmer's gondola
   C. by disguising himself as a pirate

10. Where does Rick's mother hide the tape?
    A. in Rick's sweater pocket
    B. in Kenny's book bag
    C. in the freezer

THE SCARIEST NIGHT
Betty Ren Wright

1. Who gets left behind at a gas station?
   A. Erin
   B. Cowper
   C. Rufus

2. Who asks Erin to scratch behind his left ear?
   A. stone lion
   B. stuffed bear
   C. plastic monkey

3. What does Erin enjoy that Cowper doesn't know how to do?
   A. skate boarding
   B. playing the guitar
   C. playing chess

4. Where does the family plan to go for their first family outing?
   A. lake
   B. zoo
   C. museum

5. What does Erin save Mr. Barnhart from?
   A. losing his parrot
   B. falling down the stairs
   C. kitchen fire

6. What does Cowper want to ask his parents at a seance?
   A. if they know he's done well at the piano
   B. if he can quit playing the piano
   C. if they miss him

7. What is unusual about Molly's family?
   A. they are all circus entertainers
   B. they are all cats
   C. they are 2 foot high dolls

8. When Cowper is missing where did he go?
   A. to Molly's
   B. on the ledge
   C. to the conservatory

9. What gift does Molly leave to Erin?
   A. Margaret Mary
   B. the Sailor
   C. a pink dress with ruffles

10. Why doesn't Erin go to the play with Molly?
    A. Molly died
    B. Erin got sick
    C. Cowper had a concert that evening

SCORPIONS
Walter Dean Myers

1. Why does Jamal need 2,000 dollars?
   A. to buy a car
   B. to pay for Randy's surgery
   C. to pay for Randy's appeal

2. What is physically wrong with Tito?
   A. asthma
   B. lazy eye
   C. no thumb

3. Who is always picking a fight with Jamal?
   A. Dwayne
   B. Billy
   C. Mack

4. What do Jamal and Tito talk about buying?
   A. plane
   B. boat
   C. motorcycle

5. What does Jamal enjoy doing?
   A. carving
   B. dancing
   C. drawing

6. What is Jamal's part time job?
   A. pumping gas
   B. delivering groceries
   C. cutting lawns

7. What is Randy in prison for?
   A. rape
   B. dealing drugs
   C. murder

8. Who is trying to be the scorpion leader in place of Jamal?
   A. Mack
   B. Indian
   C. Tito

9. What does Jamal do with the gun?
   A. throw it in a dumpster
   B. give it back to Mack
   C. give it to the police

10. Who shoots Angel and Indian?
    A. Tito
    B. Jamal
    C. Dwayne

THE SECRET KEEPER
Gloria Whelan

1. How does Bryce communicate with Matt?
    A. through phone calls
    B. through the personals in the newspaper
    C. he leaves notes in a tree for Annie

2. Who is a spoiled brat?
    A. Robin
    B. Matt
    C. Ed

3. What was inside the letter Bryce sent to Annie?
    A. dead orchid
    B. map
    C. picture

4. Who gives Matt a fly rod?
    A. Bryce
    B. Thomas
    C. Mr. Larimer

5. How does Matt think his mother was killed?
    A. swimming accident
    B. stabbed by thieves
    C. car accident

6. What did Annie learn about Matt's mother's death?
    A. it was faked, she's really alive
    B. she was killed by Matt's father
    C. she killed herself

7. Why was everyone out looking for Matt?
    A. he was lost
    B. he ran away
    C. he was kidnapped

8. When Matt's dad disappears what does Annie think happened?
    A. he's in California
    B. Mr. Larimer and Dr. Bradford killed him
    C. he's in jail

9. What do the Larimers want to do a few days after Annie tells them her secret?
    A. take Annie on a cruise
    B. send Annie home
    C. take Matt home

10. Who helps Annie escape when she runs away?
    A. Thomas
    B. Ed
    C. Mrs. Bradford

THE SECRET OF SANCTUARY ISLAND
A.M. Monson

1. What is Jan good at?
   A. cooking
   B. fixing cars
   C. basketball

2. Why does Jan believe Todd about how the canoe sank?
   A. because Kevin's sweat shirt was dry
   B. because Todd volunteered to show his dad the place
   C. because Todd looked terrified

3. Who runs 'Dreams Are Yours Vacations'?
   A. Baldy
   B. Chuck
   C. Mike

4. What do Kevin and Todd find on Sanctuary Island?
   A. a post card
   B. a computer printout
   C. a stereo

5. What does Todd take a picture of?
   A. the burglars
   B. Sanctuary Island
   C. boxes in a trash can

6. Who was being murdered?
   A. Mike
   B. Baldy
   C. Baldy's wife

7. Who were the burglars?
   A. Baldy and his wife
   B. Mr. and Mrs. Polaski
   C. Chuck and Mike

8. Where do Todd and Kevin think the loot is hidden?
   A. under the bridge
   B. Sanctuary Island
   C. in Baldy's house

9. How do Todd and Kevin help capture the murderers?
   A. they steal their canoe
   B. they steal their paddles
   C. they let the air out of their tires

10. What does Jan ask Todd to teach her how to do?
    A. fish
    B. play basketball
    C. ride a bike

SECRET SILENT SCREAMS
Joan Lowery Nixon

1. Who is Karen Prescott?
   A. a nosey neighbor
   B. a jealous student
   C. a police officer

2. Who murdered Barry?
   A. Emmett
   B. the Cuatros
   C. Marti

3. What is missing from Barry's room after his death?
   A. photos of the Cuatros
   B. his baseball collection
   C. his stereo system

4. What was Barry killed with?
   A. a baseball bat
   B. a gun
   C. a pillow

5. What clue lets Marti know that Barry was murdered?
   A. Barry had rope burns on his wrists
   B. a glass of milk was in his room
   C. the weapon was in the wrong hand

6. What was found at the scene of Barry's death and two other kids' suicides?
   A. hair from a blond wig
   B. video of Sudden Death by Flesh
   C. drugs

7. What does the police officer tell Marti to do?
   A. go out of town for a while
   B. tell her story to the newspaper
   C. change the locks on her home

8. Who chases and confronts Marti at school?
   A. Barry's girlfriend
   B. T.V. camera and reporters
   C. the Cuatros

9. How does the killer get his intended victims to write their suicide notes?
   A. he asks them to copy a poem
   B. he threatens to hurt their families
   C. he writes it for them

10. Who keeps following Marti?
    A. someone in a light gray car
    B. a police detective
    C. someone in a ski mask

SEND NO BLESSINGS
Phyllis Reynolds Naylor

1. Where does Harless take Beth and the children?
   A. to play miniature golf
   B. to the railroad station
   C. trick or treating

2. How come Beth has problems with typing class second semester?
   A. she can't spell
   B. she lost her typing book
   C. she lost her glasses

3. What color is Harless's hair?
   A. red
   B. brown
   C. blond

4. What does Beth make in order to earn money?
   A. clothes
   B. flowers
   C. cookies

5. What does Harless do for a living?
   A. milk cows
   B. sell grain
   C. deliver bread

6. What does Beth's father not know how to do?
   A. drive
   B. read
   C. dance

7. What does Beth's sister, Gerry, get?
   A. a job
   B. married
   C. pregnant

8. How does Beth feel about Stephanie?
   A. they are best friends
   B. she doesn't like her
   C. she is angry with her

9. What does Beth's family do with the food basket the church gives to them for Christmas?
   A. give it to the town mission
   B. eat it
   C. throw it away

10. What do Beth's parents give the older children for Christmas?
    A. encyclopedias
    B. car
    C. T.V.

THE SERPENT NEVER SLEEPS
Scott O'Dell

1. What does Countess Diana take away from Serena?
   A. her freedom
   B. her invitation
   C. the serpent ring

2. Why does Anthony flee to the New World?
   A. he killed Robert Carr's servant
   B. he threatened the king's life
   C. he stole a gold ring

3. How does Anthony Foxcroft die?
   A. drowning
   B. hangs
   C. shot

4. Who became Humility's guardian?
   A. Emma Swinton
   B. Serena
   C. Diana

5. Who proposes marriage to Serena?
   A. Marshal Dale
   B. Captain Argall
   C. Tom Barlow

6. Why did Tom Barlow become so ill?
   A. he has an infected wound from a hunting accident
   B. he was poisoned by an arrow
   C. he was poisoned by a snake bite

7. Why does Marshal Dale send Pocahontas to live with Reverend Whitaker?
   A. so she wouldn't be a temptation to the men
   B. so she could learn white men's ways
   C. so she could become a Christian

8. What does Emma Swinton give Serena as a wedding gift?
   A. a porcelain teapot
   B. curtain material
   C. a small mirror

9. Who does Pocahontas marry?
   A. John Rolfe
   B. Marshal Dale
   C. Captain Argall

10. Why do the Indians smoke out the people in Tom Barlow's house?
    A. to kidnap Pocahontas
    B. to rescue Pocahontas
    C. to kill the white men

SHADOW BROTHERS
A.E. Cannon

1. What does Diana like?
   A. red haired guys
   B. nature
   C. animals

2. What does Henry do well?
   A. write poetry
   B. sing
   C. dance

3. What do Henry and Marcus drive?
   A. a hearse
   B. a jeep
   C. a truck

4. What does Henry do after a track meet?
   A. celebrate with Marcus
   B. hit Marcus
   C. throw up

5. What is Henry's dad?
   A. fireman
   B. postal worker
   C. policeman

6. What does Henry's grandfather want him to do?
   A. stay with Marcus
   B. live with him
   C. stay with Henry's father

7. How does Henry and Marcus' double date with Celia and Diana turn out?
   A. serious
   B. funny
   C. disastrous

8. Who is Frank?
   A. Henry and Marcus' neighbor
   B. Henry and Marcus' enemy
   C. Henry and Marcus' tutor

9. Who does Diana rescue?
   A. animals
   B. swimmers
   C. babies

10. Where do Marcus and Henry work?
    A. in a movie theater
    B. in a motel
    C. at a car wash

SHANNY ON HER OWN
Lael Littke

1. What instrument does Shanny play?
   A. drums
   B. clarinet
   C. French horn

2. What does Thor write?
   A. poetry
   B. musical
   C. book

3. What does Loydene give to all the girls?
   A. tee shirts
   B. buttons
   C. ribbons

4. Who wins Pioneer Day Queen?
   A. Twyla
   B. Loydene
   C. Shanny

5. How does everyone describe Twyla?
   A. Miss Rudeness
   B. Miss Smart Mouth
   C. Miss Nice

6. Who does Aunt Adabelle talk to at the Bride's house?
   A. DeWitt
   B. Thor
   C. Uncle Vic

7. Who loves Shanny at the beginning of the story?
   A. Bucky
   B. DeWitt
   C. Thor

8. What does Shanny say whenever she gets a chance to talk to people?
   A. a riddle
   B. a joke
   C. a did you know story

9. What is Shanny's dad?
   A. a milk shake
   B. a pickle
   C. a hot dog

10. What is Loydene's favorite saying?
    A. O glory
    B. Lardy
    C. Praise be

SHARK BENEATH THE REEF
Jean Craighead George

1. What does Tomas expect to find when he climbs the volcano?
   A. temple of the gods
   B. fossils and dinosaurs
   C. ship of gold

2. What happened to Ramon, Jr., Tomas' father?
   A. killed by a shark
   B. fell into the volcano
   C. went to the mainland to live

3. Who is coming to see the fishermen?
   A. oficiales
   B. fish buyers
   C. biologists

4. Why were all the people of Colonia Zaragosa celebrating?
   A. it was the 4th of July
   B. it was the Day of No More Factory Boats
   C. they had a great catch

5. What does Jose Morellos like to do?
   A. fish
   B. repair motors
   C. make fireworks

6. What does Tomas borrow from Uncle Diaz?
   A. spear
   B. diver's mask
   C. scuba tank

7. What does Senor Fuertes say Romas should become?
   A. fisherman
   B. teacher
   C. biologist

8. How does Tomas get his hammerhead shark?
   A. spear
   B. net
   C. gun

9. Who tries to steal Tomas' hammerhead?
   A. Zoro
   B. Jose
   C. Miguel

10. What is Pebbles?
    A. sea lion
    B. dolphin
    C. dog

SING DOWN THE MOON
Scott O'Dell

1. What did Tall Boy do to get his name?
   A. tell wild stories
   B. save his village
   C. kill a bear

2. What does Bright Morning do that is wrong while tending sheep?
   A. leave the sheep in a storm
   B. allow a lamb to be attacked
   C. graze the sheep on private pasture

3. Who captures Bright Morning and Running Bird?
   A. Spaniards
   B. Utes
   C. Apaches

4. Where do Nehana, Bright Morning, and Running Bird meet to begin their escape?
   A. back alley
   B. church
   C. market

5. What is Bright Morning made to do as a slave?
   A. tend children
   B. work in the fields
   C. serve food

6. What is physically wrong with Tall Boy?
   A. he is lame
   B. his arm doesn't work
   C. he lost one eye

7. What is Bright Morning required to do during her Womanhood Ceremony?
   A. not eat for three days
   B. be silent
   C. run errands

8. Who destroyed the Navajo village?
   A. Apaches
   B. Long Knives
   C. Spaniards

9. Where is the Navajo nation taken to?
   A. Bosque Redondo
   B. Canyon de Chelly
   C. Black Mesa

10. What is Tall Boy imprisoned at the fort for doing?
    A. hitting an Apache
    B. hitting an officer
    C. hitting a slave

SINGULARITY
William Sleator

1. What do Harry and Barry find all over Uncle Ambrose' house?
   A. mounted skeletons
   B. mounds of trash
   C. expensive stones

2. What unusual thing happens inside the playhouse?
   A. people shrink in size
   B. time goes faster
   C. everything spoken comes out backwards

3. Who dies inside the playhouse?
   A. Fred
   B. Lucy
   C. Barry

4. How does Harry try to get rid of the playhouse keys?
   A. he locks them inside the playhouse
   B. he throws them in the river
   C. he melts them down in the fireplace

5. What has the Singularity been sending through?
   A. beautiful gems
   B. pictures
   C. garbage

6. How often does Harry go on Holiday while he's in the playhouse?
   A. once a week
   B. once a month
   C. once every three months

7. What happens to The Approaching One?
   A. it eats itself
   B. the police shoot it
   C. it returns to the other universe

8. How much older is Harry when he finally leaves the playhouse?
   A. one week
   B. one month
   C. one year

9. Why do the police come to the playhouse?
   A. Barry calls them
   B. they hear an explosion
   C. they heard a scream

10. What happens to the Singularity after the explosion?
    A. it is enlarged
    B. it disappears
    C. it becomes smaller

SKEETER
K. Smith

1. How does Joey hurt himself?
   A. he falls out of a tree
   B. he shoots his foot
   C. he falls over a cliff

2. What does Skeeter have Steve do with his rifle?
   A. nothing
   B. shoot Skeeter's mule
   C. kill Daryl

3. When Skeeter and the boys go deer hunting what does Steve's father make them take?
   A. stretcher
   B. tent
   C. hiker's stove

4. How did Skeeter make his living?
   A. as a handyman
   B. carving pictures on guns
   C. cleaning guns

5. What does Skeeter call Steve?
   A. Junior
   B. Master
   C. Son

6. What does Skeeter's will require the boys to do?
   A. enter a shooting contest
   B. sell his guns
   C. burn Skeeter's property

7. Why are the boys on Skeeter's property?
   A. they are lost
   B. to scare Skeeter
   C. to find a Christmas tree

8. Why does Skeeter say he needs Joey?
   A. to help him with the chores
   B. to run errands
   C. to make him laugh

9. What does Joey not have?
   A. gun
   B. hunting dog
   C. truck

10. What does Skeeter say Joey needs?
    A. courage
    B. patience
    C. skill

THE SKELETON MAN
Jay Bennett

1. What does Ray want to be?
   A. an elephant trainer
   B. a banker
   C. a lawyer

2. What does Ray's girl, Laura, like to do?
   A. play the slot machines
   B. go bowling
   C. go sky diving

3. Where does Ray work?
   A. in a diner
   B. in a department store
   C. in a garage

4. What does a gambler give Ray in exchange for nine dollars?
   A. gun
   B. medal
   C. car

5. What did Ray's uncle formerly do?
   A. doctor
   B. mechanic
   C. accountant

6. Where does Ray's father die?
   A. hospital
   B. jail
   C. cave

7. Where does Ray meet Albert Dawson?
   A. in his backyard
   B. in the cemetery
   C. in the park

8. What does Dawson do to teach Ray a lesson?
   A. beat him up
   B. shoot a cat
   C. kill his mother

9. Where is Aunt Alice found dead?
   A. closet
   B. river
   C. car

10. Who is Pete Wilson?
    A. a treasure officer
    B. the hit man
    C. the police

SLAKE'S LIMBO
Felice Holman

1. What is Slake's fantasy?
   A. his mother will come for him
   B. to drive a subway train
   C. the leaves won't fall off the trees

2. What is Slake allergic to?
   A. dope
   B. penicillin
   C. dust

3. Why don't the gangs want Slake?
   A. he is too clumsy
   B. he is too old
   C. he is too rich

4. What do a gang of boys take from Slake?
   A. lunch
   B. sweater
   C. watch

5. Before Slake ran away who did he live with?
   A. grandfather
   B. neighbor
   C. aunt

6. How was Joseph killed?
   A. subway accident
   B. hit by a truck
   C. plane crash

7. What does Willis Joe Whinny want to be?
   A. airline pilot
   B. film editor
   C. sheep rancher

8. What does Slake share his food with?
   A. roaches
   B. rat
   C. lizard

9. What does Slake not do to make money?
   A. recycle cans
   B. sell newspapers
   C. sweep floors

10. What crime does Slake commit?
    A. jumping the turnstile
    B. stealing food
    C. snatching purses

THE SLEEPWALKER
R.L. Stine

1. What does Mrs. Cottler have of Mayra's?
   A. her diary
   B. her scarf
   C. blue beads

2. What happens to Donna?
   A. she is run off the road
   B. she is burned at the stake
   C. she is accused of being a witch

3. Why is "the neck" following Mayra?
   A. he thinks she killed his brother
   B. he wants to kidnap her
   C. he wants to meet her

4. Why is Link following Mayra?
   A. he wants to scare her
   B. he wants them to get back together
   C. he thinks she is in danger

5. Why does the doctor say Mayra is sleepwalking?
   A. she wants to run away from home
   B. she is tired
   C. she is working out a problem

6. What does Walker try to do to Mayra?
   A. kiss her
   B. drown her
   C. save her

7. How does Walker keep Mayra from telling what she saw?
   A. he kidnaps her mother
   B. he threatened her
   C. he hypnotized her

8. What does Mayra remember?
   A. seeing Walker knife a hitchhiker
   B. Walker committing a hit and run
   C. seeing her old boyfriend killed

9. Who is Mrs. Cottler?
   A. a professor of occult studies
   B. a witch
   C. a writer of mysteries

10. Who saved Mayra from Walker?
    A. Hazel, the cat
    B. Link
    C. the neck

SNIPER

Theodore Taylor

1. What does Ben's mother say about Ben in a letter to his grandmother?
   A. Ben is stupid and mediocre
   B. Ben is playing football
   C. Ben is on the student council

2. What does Ben's mother do for a living?
   A. model
   B. photographer
   C. teacher

3. What does Ben's father use to control the cats?
   A. fire extinguisher
   B. gun
   C. whip

4. Who is Rocky?
   A. Ben's cousin
   B. Ben's lion
   C. Ben's girlfriend

5. What happens to the sisters, Helen and Daisy?
   A. they run away
   B. they were treed
   C. they are shot to death

6. In Africa, who attacks Ben's parents?
   A. wild animals
   B. the natives
   C. poachers

7. What disaster threatened the cat compound?
   A. fire
   B. flood
   C. earthquake

8. What kind of fence was put up around the grounds?
   A. brick
   B. stockade
   C. bamboo

9. Why was the sniper killing the animals?
   A. for sport
   B. for revenge
   C. for target practice

10. Where is Ben when he recognizes the sniper?
    A. church
    B. McDonalds
    C. Laundromat

SNOW BOUND

Harry Mazer

1. Why does Tony's father get rid of the dog?
   A. he's too expensive
   B. he chewed the rug
   C. he barked at night

2. What gets frostbit?
   A. Lucy's right foot
   B. Lucy's nose
   C. Lucy's fingers

3. What does Tony find in the trunk to eat?
   A. hardened peanut butter sandwich
   B. moldy orange
   C. leather belt

4. What food does Cindy share with Tony while they are stranded?
   A. beef jerky
   B. chocolate chip cookies
   C. saltines

5. What does Cindy want to do in the car to stay warm?
   A. wrap herself in road maps
   B. cut up and wear the seat covers
   C. build a fire

6. What does Cindy drink out of?
   A. hub cap
   B. ashtray
   C. flashlight

7. What does Tony make a knife out of?
   A. can opener
   B. nail
   C. fingernail file

8. What does Lucy do to pass time while Tony is gone?
   A. make up songs
   B. start a journal
   C. study algebra

9. What wild animals confront Tony?
   A. dogs
   B. lions
   C. bears

10. How many days were Tony and Lucy gone?
    A. 11
    B. 20
    C. 5

THE SNOWMAN
R.L. Stine

1. What does Heather dream about?
   A. ways to kill her uncle
   B. leaving home
   C. being married to Ben

2. What does Heather's uncle enjoy doing?
   A. playing golf
   B. embarrassing Heather in front of her friends
   C. telling Heather how much he cares about her

3. What does Heather loan Snowman?
   A. $2,000
   B. her car
   C. her coat

4. What does Snowman's brother need?
   A. clothes for school
   B. an operation
   C. braces

5. Who does Snowman kill?
   A. Heather
   B. Ben
   C. Heather's uncle

6. What does Snowman kill with?
   A. gun
   B. knife
   C. scarf

7. How did Snowman try to kill Heather?
   A. smother her inside a snowman
   B. set her on fire
   C. drug her

8. How did she escape from Snowman finally?
   A. she kicked him and ran
   B. she threw dirt in his eyes and ran
   C. she set him on fire and ran

9. What happened to the check in Snowman's pocket?
   A. it gets lost
   B. it gets burned up
   C. it gets cashed

10. Why is the FBI looking for Snowman?
    A. he kidnapped a child
    B. he killed his father
    C. he robbed a liquor store

SOMETHING UPSTAIRS
Avi

1. What does Kenny take to the pharmacist to have tested?
    A. a stain on a splinter
    B. a glass of wine
    C. a jar of powder

2. What does Caleb want Kenny to do?
    A. leave his house
    B. find his murderer
    C. play with him

3. What does Willinghast take away from Kenny?
    A. a key chain
    B. a gun
    C. Caleb

4. What is Caleb always doing in the attic room?
    A. looking for a weapon
    B. looking for a way out
    C. trying to scare Kenny

5. What does the first microfilm Kenny reads say about Caleb?
    A. he was murdered
    B. he was an escaped slave
    C. he committed suicide

6. What does the second microfilm say about Caleb?
    A. he was murdered
    B. he committed suicide
    C. he was an escaped slave

7. What does Willinghast want Henry to do?
    A. murder Caleb
    B. return to the 20th century
    C. bring Caleb to him

8. What happens if Henry gets hurt or loses something while in the past?
    A. he will die
    B. he will change the future
    C. he will haunt the past forever

9. Who killed Caleb the first time?
    A. Seagrave
    B. Willinghast
    C. Ormsbee

10. What happened as a result of Caleb being stoned?
    A. he is blind in one eye
    B. he is deaf in one ear
    C. he is crippled

SOMETHING'S ROTTEN IN THE STATE OF MARYLAND
Laura A. Sonnemark

1. Where are Simon and Marie going when they have an accident?
   A. a restaurant
   B. a football game
   C. to buy material

2. What happens to Brian?
   A. he breaks his leg
   B. he drops out of school
   C. he runs away

3. What does Marie spend her spare time watching?
   A. Santa Barbara
   B. cartoons
   C. people

4. What does Marie's family like to do?
   A. laugh
   B. argue
   C. sell antiques

5. Who is Brian?
   A. Marie's brother
   B. Marie's neighbor
   C. Marie's boyfriend

6. How does Brian feel about Marie working on the play?
   A. he thinks its great
   B. he hates it
   C. he doesn't care

7. How do three characters in the play die?
   A. poison
   B. sword
   C. drowning

8. How does the play turn out?
   A. its a flop
   B. its a big success
   C. its expensive

9. Who sends Marie a dozen carnations?
   A. Simon
   B. her mother
   C. the director

10. What is the water in the play made out of?
    A. blue material
    B. colored foil
    C. styrofoam

SONG OF THE BUFFALO BOY
Sherry Garland

1. What does Loi do at her engagement party to disgrace herself?
   A. she is rude to Officer Hiep and his mother
   B. she refuses Officer Hiep's gifts
   C. she ruins the food and her clothes

2. How does Loi fake her death?
   A. she pretends to drown
   B. she pretends to be run over by a water buffalo
   C. she pretends to fall over a cliff

3. What does Khai make to sell?
   A. carvings
   B. pottery
   C. bone jewelry

4. Who helps Loi survive in Ho Chi Minh City?
   A. Raymond Smith
   B. Joe
   C. Quy

5. What does Joe do to try to make himself look part American?
   A. hold his eyes open wider
   B. look people in the eye
   C. dye his hair orange

6. Why does Loi need a doctor?
   A. she has food poisoning
   B. she cut her foot
   C. she has a high fever

7. Where does Loi live while in Ho Chi Minh City?
   A. Buddhist temple
   B. a back alley
   C. Amerasian Park

8. What does Loi learn about the man in her photo?
   A. he's her father
   B. he was a helpful stranger
   C. he was her mother's lover

9. Who does Loi eventually marry?
   A. Khai
   B. Joe
   C. Officer Hiep

10. Who does Raymond Smith take to America?
    A. Joe
    B. Loi
    C. Khai

S.O.R. LOSERS
Avi

1. Why was Ed made the goalie?
   A. he was tallest
   B. he was fastest
   C. he was strongest

2. Why did Mr. Lester call Ed to his room the day after their first game?
   A. to discuss soccer strategy
   B. to make Ed team captain
   C. to check on team morale

3. Who volunteers to be the soccer coach?
   A. Mr. Lester
   B. Mr. Tillman
   C. Mr. Sullivan

4. Who does Ed meet behind the garbage bins at lunch?
   A. Saltz
   B. Lucy Neblet
   C. Radosh

5. What does Ed ask all the team members to give him?
   A. their best effort
   B. their vote of confidence
   C. their team shirts

6. What does their coach give examples from when explaining not giving up?
   A. past school games
   B. his personal experience
   C. war stories

7. How many games did the team win?
   A. 0
   B. 1
   C. 2

8. What was the team given when the school was afraid their attitude would affect the other teams?
   A. a pep talk
   B. their own dressing room
   C. their own bus

9. Who were the team members sent to because of their attitude?
   A. a local minister
   B. Mr. Tillman, the counselor
   C. Ms. Appleton

10. Who is Lucy Neblet?
    A. Ed's girlfriend
    B. Ed's history project partner
    C. Ed's sister

THE SPANISH KIDNAPPING DISASTER
Mary Downing Hahn

1. What are Amy and Felix looking for when they realize they can't see their parents?
   A. book of Spanish phrases
   B. souvenirs
   C. Amy's barrette

2. How does Grace respond when she is asked where she is from?
   A. I am a citizen of the world
   B. I am from the wind and sea
   C. I am not of this world

3. What does Grace offer to show the family?
   A. windmills
   B. castles
   C. works of art

4. Where do the kidnappers take Amy, Philip, and Felix?
   A. to a camper
   B. to a cave
   C. to a farm

5. What does Orlando take away from Amy, Philip, and Felix?
   A. their shoes
   B. their jewelry
   C. their passports

6. What does Grace want to do with the ransom money?
   A. use it to save the whales
   B. use it to feed the starving children
   C. use it to help overthrow the government

7. What do the children eat while captive?
   A. wild jack rabbit
   B. canned beans
   C. goat stew

8. Who learned some Spanish?
   A. Amy
   B. Philip
   C. Felix

9. Who gets shot?
   A. Grace
   B. Orlando
   C. Charles

10. What does Grace give to Felix in the hospital?
    A. gold hoop earrings
    B. her address
    C. flowers

THE SPANISH SMILE
Scott O'Dell

1. What did Lucinda's father make her wear the only time he let her visit her grandmother?
   A. her mother's pearls
   B. a formal dress
   C. handcuffs

2. What does Don Enrique throw out of Lucinda's window?
   A. record player
   B. radio
   C. television

3. Where does Lucinda go dressed as a maid?
   A. to the infanta
   B. into town
   C. into the crypt

4. What does Christopher Dawson find in a room under the castle?
   A. a dungeon with prisoners
   B. crystal coffins
   C. a fortune in gold and jewels

5. What does Don Enrique give each woman before he has them killed?
   A. a kiss
   B. a white dress and slippers
   C. gold bar and pearl choker

6. What does Don Enrique plan to capture?
   A. the U.S. treasury building
   B. an atomic plant
   C. the naval base

7. How is Don Enrique killed?
   A. heart attack
   B. pushed out of a tower window
   C. bushmaster snake bite

8. What did Lucinda find when she had the wall in front of the clothes press removed?
   A. the body of her mother and her lover
   B. clothes
   C. the body of John Wesley Blake

9. What were Captain Wolfe and Dr. Wolfe?
   A. Nazi war criminals
   B. escaped convicts
   C. jewel thieves

10. What does Lucinda get that has always been forbidden on the island?
    A. newspaper
    B. car
    C. radio

THE SQUEAKY WHEEL
R. Smith

1. What nationality is Mark's best friend, Joe?
   A. Russian
   B. Mexican
   C. Chinese

2. What does Mark's father bring him?
   A. his bike
   B. his football
   C. his winter coat

3. What is Phil known as?
   A. the school's bully
   B. a whiz kid
   C. the ace athlete

4. What does Phil's sister paint?
   A. pictures of mountains
   B. Mark's fingernails
   C. her bedroom wall

5. What contest does Mark win at a birthday party?
   A. the three legged race
   B. arm wrestling
   C. foul shots

6. What meal do Mark and his father eat out every Sunday for?
   A. lunch
   B. breakfast
   C. dinner

7. What holiday do Mark and his mom and dad celebrate together?
   A. Easter
   B. Christmas
   C. Thanksgiving

8. What is Phil arrested for?
   A. murder
   B. shoplifting
   C. armed robbery

9. What do the girls call Mark?
   A. a hunk
   B. a monster
   C. a jerk

10. What does Phil call Mark?
   A. the one dollar friend
   B. an old buddy
   C. a nerd

THE STALKER
Joan Lowery Nixon

1. What was Stella Trax murdered with?
   A. Bobbie's scarf
   B. an axe
   C. a book end

2. What is missing from Bobbie's house?
   A. money
   B. pictures
   C. a diary

3. Where did Stella Trax work?
   A. La Salon
   B. K-mart
   C. Texaco

4. Where had Elton been living?
   A. on a farm
   B. in a prison
   C. in France

5. What is Daryl known for?
   A. his temper
   B. his laziness
   C. doing drugs

6. How did Bobbie learn of her mother's death?
   A. T.V.
   B. police
   C. Jennifer

7. Where does Jennifer find Bobbie after her mother is killed?
   A. beach shack
   B. at the park
   C. behind her house

8. What does Stella keep hidden under the board in her kitchen cabinet?
   A. drugs
   B. a gun
   C. her purse

9. What crime was Stella involved in?
   A. blackmail
   B. counterfeiting credit cards
   C. prostitution

10. Who is the murderer?
    A. Elton
    B. Biddle
    C. Daryl

STAR BABY
Joan Lowery Nixon

1. How does Johnny rescue Abby from having to perform at a birthday party?
    A. spills punch on her
    B. takes her for a long walk
    C. pushes her into a pool

2. What does Mrs. Fitch think she is seeing through the trees?
    A. spy's signal lights
    B. a mugging
    C. Abby taking a walk

3. What does Abby's mother make her wear everywhere?
    A. a pink dress
    B. a Shirley Temple wig
    C. her tap shoes

4. What is Bobby doing when Abby picks him up at the auditions?
    A. arguing with the director
    B. gambling
    C. sleeping

5. What do Luke's parents give him permission to do?
    A. drop out of school
    B. get married
    C. join the navy

6. When Abby goes to see acting agent, Mr. Harkens, what does he tell her?
    A. she is going to be famous again
    B. she has no looks or body
    C. she's too old

7. What does Abby do on stage to get Mr. Perkins to choose her?
    A. show some of her leg
    B. wink at him
    C. make her skirt fall down

8. What is Abby good at?
    A. singing
    B. comedy
    C. dancing

9. Who is Abby's mother having an affair with?
    A. Al, the agent
    B. Mr. Harkens
    C. Pat Perkins

10. What does Abby's mother do to her dad when he is having a heart attack?
    A. slap him
    B. hold him
    C. give him aspirin

STONE WORDS
Pam Conrad

1. How does Zoe's mother pick out Zoe's name?
   A. from a book of names
   B. it's her mother's friend's name
   C. from a grave stone

2. Besides Zoe, who else can see Zoe Louise?
   A. Oscar
   B. PopPop
   C. Grandma

3. What does Zoe find in the woods?
   A. rose bushes
   B. a ghost child
   C. snakes

4. Why does Zoe Louise always look in Zoe's eyes?
   A. to see if she is lying
   B. to see if she knows how she died
   C. to keep from being afraid

5. What is wrong with Zoe's play house?
   A. everything has been torn up
   B. the furniture is upside down on the ceiling
   C. there are no toys in it

6. What is Zoe Louise's father going to bring her for her birthday?
   A. puppy
   B. pony
   C. china doll

7. What does Zoe find in the basement?
   A. Zoe Louise's old toys
   B. a portrait of Zoe Louise
   C. old newspapers

8. Who does Zoe Louise run away with as she is rotting?
   A. PopPop
   B. Oscar
   C. Grandma

9. How does Zoe Louise die?
   A. kitchen fire
   B. fell from a horse
   C. cliff gives way

10. After Zoe saves Zoe Louise what does Zoe find in the woods?
    A. raspberry bushes
    B. a wild pony
    C. an old grave

STRANGE ATTRACTORS
William Sleator

1. Where does Silvan hide the device everyone is looking for?
   A. in Max' jacket pocket
   B. in Max' book bag
   C. in Max' waist pouch

2. What does the real Eve ask Max to bring to her?
   A. his jacket
   B. a receipt
   C. the phaser

3. What does Max have to do for the imposter in order to be allowed to keep his phaser?
   A. register Eve and Sylvan
   B. send a time line to chaos
   C. kill the real Eve and Sylvan

4. Where do the impostors take Max to hide out?
   A. 3,025 A.D.
   B. 33,019 B.C.
   C. 1845 A.D.

5. Where do the impostors take Max for a surprise treat?
   A. Spain
   B. Arctic Circle
   C. Bangkok

6. Where does Sylvan, the imposter, threaten to send Max?
   A. to chaos
   B. to the end of time
   C. the molten earth

7. Where do the impostors send Eve, Sylvan and Max?
   A. to chaos
   B. inside a tree
   C. to molten earth

8. Who sends the imposter, Sylvan, to his death in molten earth?
   A. the real Sylvan
   B. Max
   C. his daughter, Eve

9. Where do Sylvan and Eve hide their second phaser?
   A. in the freezer
   B. inside a teddy bear
   C. inside Max's jacket

10. What do Sylvan and Eve do when caught in Eve and Max's headlights?
    A. shoot
    B. freeze
    C. run

THE STRANGE CASE OF THE RELUCTANT PARTNERS
Mark Geller

1. What is Elaine always seen doing?
   A. reading a book
   B. polishing her nails
   C. gossiping and giggling

2. What kind of personality does Elaine have?
   A. funny
   B. sarcastic
   C. boring

3. What does Elaine say her father is?
   A. poet
   B. banker
   C. electrician

4. What do Elaine and Thomas have in common?
   A. divorced parents
   B. Sherlock Holmes mysteries
   C. tennis

5. What are Elaine's family?
   A. refugees
   B. Presbyterian
   C. vegetarian

6. How come Elaine's family doesn't own a car?
   A. they are too poor
   B. they can't drive
   C. they don't believe in them

7. What does Elaine teach Thomas about?
   A. flowers
   B. archery
   C. sculpture

8. What does Elaine do when Thomas reads her biography aloud in class?
   A. she cries
   B. she defends herself
   C. nothing, she's speechless

9. What is Thomas' opinion of Brigette?
   A. she is classy and sophisticated
   B. she is vain, spoiled and shallow
   C. she is boring

10. What do they do the first time Thomas goes to Elaine's house?
    A. fall in love
    B. insult each other
    C. tell their most embarrassing moment

STRIDER
Beverly Cleary

1. Who gets custody of the dog?
   A. Leigh and Kevin
   B. Strider and Leigh
   C. Barry and Leigh

2. What words does Strider learn to read?
   A. sit and stay
   B. attack and heal
   C. roll over

3. What is stuck all over a wall in Barry's kitchen?
   A. spaghetti
   B. gum
   C. spider webs

4. What does Strider fetch for Barry?
   A. tennis balls
   B. golf balls
   C. racket balls

5. Who does Barry almost always see on the beach?
   A. Miss America
   B. Mr. Pizza
   C. Mr. President

6. What does Leigh's father lose?
   A. sports car
   B. tracker trailer rig
   C. Harley cycle

7. What does Leigh call his home?
   A. mansion
   B. prison
   C. shack

8. What does Leigh ask his father to build for him?
   A. dog house
   B. fence
   C. tree house

9. What do Leigh and Geneva do on their first date?
   A. pull weeds
   B. wash Strider
   C. wax the car

10. What does Geneva give to Leigh?
    A. her hair
    B. her false eye lashes
    C. her nail clippings

SUCH NICE KIDS

Eve Bunting

1. What does Jason give to Destiny as a birthday present?
   A. a stuffed animal
   B. a book of poetry
   C. a crystal rose

2. What happened to Pidge?
   A. he got killed
   B. he was kicked out of school
   C. he moved away

3. What did Meek do with his father's gun?
   A. rob a convenience store
   B. shoot at birds
   C. clean it

4. Where were Jason's parents?
   A. at a church social
   B. on a business trip
   C. at work

5. What did Jason need $950 for?
   A. to buy drugs
   B. to get a used car
   C. to get his mother's car fixed

6. What part time job do Pidge and Jason have?
   A. they work at the hardware store
   B. they park cars
   C. they wash cars

7. What is Meeker's father known for?
   A. gambling
   B. rescuing swimmers
   C. lying

8. Who thinks everything is a thrill and big joke?
   A. Pidge
   B. Meek
   C. Jason's parents

9. Who tried to get help?
   A. Jason
   B. Pidge
   C. Meek

10. What is buried with Pidge?
    A. a crystal rose
    B. the gun
    C. the money

SUMMER OF THE MONKEYS
Wilson Rawls

1. What is Sally Gooden?
   A. dog
   B. monkey
   C. cow

2. What will the circus pay for all of the monkeys but one?
   A. two dollars each
   B. five dollars each
   C. seven dollars each

3. What does Jay Berry use for bait in his traps?
   A. apples
   B. corn
   C. bread

4. What does Jay Berry catch in his net?
   A. chicken
   B. goose
   C. rabbit

5. What does Jay Berry lose when he is drunk?
   A. net
   B. dog
   C. britches

6. What does Grandpa buy after leaving the library?
   A. chicken wire
   B. coconuts
   C. dart gun

7. What does Daisy find after the storm?
   A. hurt dove
   B. double rainbow
   C. fairy ring

8. Who does Jay Berry pray to?
   A. The Spirit of the Hills
   B. The Man of the Mountains
   C. Jesus

9. What does Daisy bring back from Oklahoma City for Jay Berry?
   A. .22 rifle
   B. sling shot
   C. britches

10. What is the one request Daisy asks of Jay Berry upon returning home?
    A. that he run with her
    B. that she ride Dolly
    C. that he teach her to catch monkeys

SUSANNA SIEGELBAUM GIVES UP GUYS
June Foley

1. What is Susanna's favorite book?
   A. Wuthering Heights
   B. The Outsiders
   C. Little Women

2. Who does Ben pretend to be?
   A. Susanna's brother
   B. Susanna's boyfriend
   C. Susanna's cousin

3. What is the only thing Ben is interested in?
   A. sports
   B. writing
   C. girls

4. What do Susanna and Ben name synonyms for?
   A. terms of endearment
   B. vomit
   C. school food

5. What happens the first time Susanna and Ben go rowing?
   A. they get lost
   B. they lose the paddles
   C. Susanna falls in the water

6. What is Susanna's volunteer job?
   A. working at the hospital
   B. tutoring kids at school
   C. working at the library

7. Who is Ben's mother?
   A. a famous author
   B. a famous singer
   C. a famous actress

8. What surprises Ben about Susanna's dad?
   A. he has hair to his waist
   B. he backpacks
   C. he bakes bread

9. What does Ben's mother tell her about Ben?
   A. he used to be in special education
   B. he learned to read at the age of three
   C. he has written a book

10. What does Susanna have to do if she looses the bet with Cassidy?
    A. help Cassidy with her homework for two months
    B. babysit Cassidy's sisters for a year
    C. wax Cassidy's car

SWEET BELLS JANGLED OUT OF TUNE
Robin F. Brancato

1. What did Eva do that causes Ellen to not be allowed to see her?
   A. she took Ellen from school without telling anyone
   B. she allowed a child to wander off
   C. she had blackouts and hallucinations

2. What is wrong with Eva's house?
   A. the windows are broken
   B. the utilities are turned off
   C. there is no furniture

3. What do Josie and Ellen bring Eva?
   A. food
   B. money
   C. clothing

4. What does Eva do to Josie?
   A. slap her
   B. close her up in the wardrobe
   C. leave her in the outhouse

5. What game does Buddha teach Ben, Ellen, and Josie to play?
   A. spin the bottle
   B. dead man's dare
   C. quarters

6. What does the note say that Ellen finds when she arrives home?
   A. the police are searching for her
   B. to not leave the house
   C. her grandfather is in the hospital

7. What does Ellen tour?
   A. the psychiatric ward
   B. the state school
   C. the penitentiary

8. What does Eva try to do to her house?
   A. fix it up
   B. sell it
   C. burn it down

9. How does Ellen get into Eva's boarded up house?
   A. through a broken window
   B. down the chimney
   C. through the dog's door

10. What does Ellen keep hidden from her mother for 7 years?
    A. her grandmother's diary
    B. a stolen purple ring
    C. the name of her kidnapper

TAKING SIDES
Gary Soto

1. What does Tony show Lincoln at a thrift shop?
   A. Lincoln's stolen TV
   B. Lincoln's stolen stereo
   C. Lincoln's stolen 10-speed

2. Who does Lincoln like?
   A. Vicky
   B. Monica
   C. Susan

3. What do Lincoln and Monica do on their first date?
   A. play basketball
   B. go to a movie
   C. eat pizza

4. Who is Lincoln's new friend?
   A. Tony
   B. James
   C. Flaco

5. How does Flaco get hurt?
   A. hit by a car
   B. beat up by a gang
   C. run over by a motorcycle

6. Why does Lincoln stay home from school?
   A. flu
   B. chicken pox
   C. hurt knee

7. Where do Lincoln and Monica always meet to talk?
   A. library
   B. bleachers
   C. cafeteria

8. Who wins the basketball game?
   A. Columbus
   B. they tied
   C. Franklin

9. Who rescues Lincoln from Coach Yesutis?
   A. Flaco
   B. Roy
   C. Tony

10. What does Lincoln eat at James' house?
    A. veal
    B. venison
    C. grits

THAT WAS THEN, THIS IS NOW
S.E. Hinton

1. Who seems to be able to get away with anything?
    A. Curtis
    B. Charlie
    C. Mark

2. What does Bryon do to get money?
    A. hustle pool
    B. pick pockets
    C. play poker

3. What does Mark steal that causes the principal to call the police?
    A. principal's car
    B. school computer
    C. fund raiser money

4. Who does Bryon like?
    A. Cissy
    B. Cathy
    C. Angela

5. Who gets shot to death?
    A. Ponyboy
    B. Mark
    C. Charlie

6. What is Cathy's brother's nickname?
    A. Coco
    B. M & M
    C. Hershey

7. How does Mark get back at Angela for what she did to him and Curtis?
    A. he ruined her clothes
    B. he threw dye on her skin
    C. he cut her hair off

8. Where do Bryon and Cathy find M & M?
    A. drainage ditch
    B. hippie house
    C. police station

9. Where does Mark hide his drugs?
    A. under his mattress
    B. in the toilet tank
    C. in the lining of his jacket

10. Who turns Mark in for selling drugs?
    A. Bryon
    B. Cathy
    C. M & M

THERE'S A GIRL IN MY HAMMERLOCK
Jerry Spinelli

1. Who is Maisie's favorite TV wrestler?
   A. Washerwoman
   B. Ma Barker
   C. The Floozie

2. At what weight does Maisie wrestle?
   A. 70 pounds
   B. 105 pounds
   C. 130 pounds

3. Who is Bernadette?
   A. rat
   B. dog
   C. snake

4. When the team only pretends to wrestle Maisie, what does she request?
   A. the hammerlock
   B. the nutcracker
   C. the squeeze

5. Which wrestler was Maisie's friend from the beginning?
   A. Eric Delong
   B. Mike Kruko
   C. George Bamberger

6. Who helped Maisie in the locker room when she was hurt?
   A. Lizard Lampley
   B. Holly Gish
   C. Tina McIntire

7. What does Maisie wear to weigh in at the first match?
   A. her grandmother's swim suit
   B. her gym suit
   C. her underwear

8. Who is the new mat maid for the wrestlers?
   A. Tina McIntire
   B. Holly Gish
   C. Lizard Lampley

9. How many matches did Maisie win?
   A. 1
   B. 0
   C. 2

10. What did Maisie rescue Frank from?
    A. house fire
    B. snow plow
    C. mad dog

THE THIRD EYE
Lois Duncan

1. What was Karen doing when Bobby disappeared?
   A. babysitting him
   B. on a date
   C. at home asleep

2. Where was Bobby found?
   A. in the woods
   B. in a car trunk
   C. at a neighbors

3. What does Karen work on?
   A. the prom committee
   B. the science fair project
   C. the homecoming float

4. What is Officer Ron Wilson afraid of?
   A. snakes
   B. dogs
   C. worms

5. What does Karen know happened to Carla?
   A. kidnapped
   B. fell into a well
   C. fell into river and drowned

6. What does Tim ask Karen to imagine?
   A. who he will marry
   B. what job he will get
   C. answers to a test

7. What happens when Tim learns Karen is psychic?
   A. he dumps her
   B. he's embarrassed for her
   C. he thinks its cool

8. Where does Karen work for the summer?
   A. at a restaurant
   B. in a home babysitting
   C. in a day care center

9. How does Karen escape when she is kidnapped?
   A. by screaming to signal help
   B. by setting off the smoke alarm
   C. by crashing through a glass door

10. Who is the child that keeps warning Karen of danger?
    A. Matthew
    B. Karen's unborn child
    C. the dead child

THIS PLACE HAS NO ATMOSPHERE
Paula Danziger

1. What does Aurora want to be when she grows up?
   A. a housewife
   B. a nurse
   C. an actress

2. What does Aurora's grandmother send them?
   A. brownies
   B. pictures
   C. toys

3. What community project do Aurora and Hal do?
   A. a community play
   B. get people to donate blood
   C. help paint the community center

4. What are Aurora's parents?
   A. vegetarians
   B. doctors
   C. animal lovers

5. On earth, what are Aurora and her friends called?
   A. pea pods
   B. radishes
   C. turnips

6. What is Aurora's school service project?
   A. to grade papers
   B. to work with the eaglettes
   C. to answer the phones

7. What do the people on the colony get to do twice a week?
   A. see a movie
   B. have a dance
   C. take a shower

8. On earth, where is the zoo located?
   A. in a stadium
   B. in the mall
   C. in the park

9. What can Aurora do at the end of one year?
   A. go back to earth
   B. live on Mars
   C. fly a rocket

10. How many years are Aurora's parents to live on the moon?
    A. five
    B. ten
    C. twenty

THROW A HUNGRY LOOP
Dona Schenker

1. What does Tack put on his windshield that he says will keep him from getting a speeding ticket?
   A. a flashing light
   B. a support your police bumper sticker
   C. a horny toad

2. Where does Tres live?
   A. Slaughter Creek Ranch
   B. Draco Ranch
   C. Taylor Horse Ranch

3. Where does Tres get the money to buy a horse?
   A. he sells his calf and heifer
   B. he breaks horses
   C. he works in town

4. What is Sissy Belle?
   A. horse
   B. mule
   C. dog

5. Who always manages to cheer Tres up?
   A. Junior
   B. Tack
   C. Robin

6. What does Tres have to do that embarrasses him?
   A. ask Robin for a date
   B. clean the stable in front of Robin
   C. ride a mule to town

7. What is wrong with the heifer?
   A. broken leg
   B. crazy from eating loco weed
   C. snake bit

8. What does Junior want to buy?
   A. a stud bull
   B. Pop's Cafe
   C. a new truck

9. What does Junior do at the dance when he is drunk?
   A. sing on stage
   B. kiss the women
   C. throw up on Tres

10. Where does the heifer calve?
    A. in a snow storm
    B. in the barn
    C. at the river

THE TORMENTERS
Lynn Hall

1. What is Sox' mother afraid of?
    A. the police
    B. dogs
    C. her son

2. Where does Heidi prefer to drink from?
    A. the kiddie pool
    B. the toilet
    C. the water dish

3. Where does Sox find dogs being trained?
    A. Guardian Angel Kennels
    B. Marnie's Pet Training School
    C. Paw Prints

4. What color truck was Sox following?
    A. blue
    B. red
    C. yellow

5. What does Monte have in the squirt gun he gives to Sox?
    A. beer
    B. ink
    C. ammonia

6. What does Valerian send Monte out for?
    A. tranquilizers
    B. mail
    C. blue slips

7. How come Valerian couldn't sell the white shepherd?
    A. he had a tatoo
    B. he was wounded in training
    C. he died

8. What was Monte being held without bail for?
    A. animal abuse
    B. mail fraud
    C. kidnapping a child

9. Why was Sox in the hospital?
    A. he had rabies
    B. he had a concussion and a broken ankle
    C. he was mauled by a dog

10. How did the police locate Heidi?
    A. Monte told where she was
    B. through a letter of complaint
    C. through a sales slip

TOURNAMENT UPSTART
Thomas J. Dygard

1. Where does the team sleep during the state tournament?
   A. on the basketball court
   B. in a motel
   C. at Floyd's home

2. Where does Jimmy get a call from?
   A. his home
   B. Saudi Arabia
   C. the president of the United States

3. What does Jimmy call one of the students?
   A. a guy in farmer clothes
   B. a pest
   C. a hateful snob

4. Why do the citizens of Cedar Grove think Floyd Bentley wants his team in the class A tournament?
   A. because they're so good
   B. so he can get a better job offer
   C. so the school will attract players

5. What does the team do to Jimmy during the tournament?
   A. hide his uniform
   B. give him a cold shower
   C. freeze him out

6. What does Big John bring to the locker room the last night of the tournament?
   A. the trophy
   B. the police
   C. letter jackets

7. Why does Big John say that Floyd is taking the team to the tournament?
   A. to embarrass them
   B. to show off the team
   C. for the experience

8. What does Jimmy talk about most?
   A. his girl
   B. his fancy car
   C. his old school and team

9. How many tickets does Big John order for the championship game?
   A. none
   B. 400
   C. 4

10. What kind of game do the Falcons play?
    A. passing game
    B. running game
    C. bad game

TRACKER
Gary Paulsen

1. How does John feel about doing chores?
   A. hates them
   B. enjoys them
   C. they're ok

2. Where are John's parents?
   A. dead and buried
   B. at work
   C. on a business trip

3. What was John throwing from the back of the team?
   A. manure
   B. seed
   C. hay

4. Why does John's grandfather hunt?
   A. for sport
   B. for meat
   C. to be a man

5. Where does John hunt?
   A. along the river
   B. in the woods
   C. edge of the swamp

6. Where does John live?
   A. in the city
   B. on a farm
   C. in the mountains

7. What kept John from shooting the doe when she stood still?
   A. he was afraid
   B. he couldn't see her clearly
   C. he knew the doe knew him

8. What did John do when it was dark?
   A. sleep
   B. track the doe
   C. build a fire

9. What does John want to do to the deer?
   A. touch it
   B. capture it
   C. kill it

10. What does John leave behind in a tree?
    A. his rifle
    B. his food
    C. his pack

TRICK OR TREAT
Richie Tankersley Cusick

1. Where does Blake kiss Martha?
   A. hayloft
   B. tree house
   C. behind the house

2. Who is the murderer?
   A. Blake
   B. Wynn
   C. Dennis

3. What does Conor find in the house?
   A. secret passages
   B. an old doll
   C. a skeleton

4. Where are Martha and Conor's parents?
   A. locked in the basement
   B. working honeymoon in Hawaii
   C. tied up out back

5. What does Conor do well?
   A. wrestle
   B. hunt
   C. cook

6. What does Greg do?
   A. teach Sunday School
   B. radio announcer
   C. guidance counselor

7. Where was Martha when the lights went out and she was being stalked?
   A. in school
   B. in the supermarket
   C. in the library

8. Why is everyone quiet around Martha?
   A. her mother was killed
   B. they are afraid of her
   C. she resembles Elizabeth

9. At the Halloween dance, what does Blake come dressed as?
   A. clown
   B. death
   C. witch

10. Who does Wynn say she saw at the dance?
    A. Martha
    B. Dennis
    C. Greg

THE TROUBLE WITH LEMONS
Daniel Hayes

1. What is Tyler good at?
   A. computers
   B. dancing
   C. running

2. How does Tyler's father die?
   A. plane crash
   B. hit and run accident
   C. heart attack

3. Who does Tyler get in a fight with?
   A. Beaver
   B. Lymie
   C. Chuckie

4. What is Tyler's medical problem?
   A. bad heart
   B. asthma
   C. epilepsy

5. What do Tyler's mother and brother do?
   A. make telephone sales
   B. work the assembly line
   C. make movies

6. What does Chuckie do when Tyler wets his pants?
   A. throws him in the shower
   B. throws him in the sprinkler
   C. throws him in the pool

7. Why is Tyler always in trouble in his science class?
   A. he talks constantly
   B. he never does his homework
   C. he keeps falling asleep

8. Where does Boo Boo die?
   A. quarry
   B. school pool
   C. principal's pool

9. Who goes to the police?
   A. Jack
   B. Mark
   C. Lymie

10. Who threw Boo Boo's body into the quarry?
    A. Jack and Mark
    B. Jack and Chuckie
    C. Bust and Mark

THE TRUE CONFESSIONS OF CHARLOTTE DOYLE
Avi

1. What does the captain tell Charlotte is the sign of a mutiny?
    A. a round robin
    B. the crew gathered in small groups
    C. cuts on the men from an oath in blood

2. Who is the stowaway?
    A. Barlow
    B. Cranick
    C. Grimes

3. Who does the captain have horse whipped?
    A. Zachariah
    B. Ewing
    C. Grimes

4. Why does the captain turn against Charlotte?
    A. she aids the crew during the mutiny
    B. she cut his face with his own whip
    C. she spit on him in front of the crew

5. Who is Charlotte accused of murdering?
    A. Mr. Keetch
    B. Mr. Fisk
    C. Mr. Hollybrass

6. What is the test the crew gives to Charlotte?
    A. to give her their plans and see if she tells
    B. to steal rum from the captain's table
    C. to climb to the top of the royal yard arm

7. Why doesn't the crew help Charlotte at the trial?
    A. they are covering for Zachariah
    B. they don't like her
    C. they think she is guilty

8. What does Charlotte sneak into the captain's cabin to get?
    A. the guns
    B. his whip
    C. a key

9. How is Captain Jaggery killed?
    A. he is shot
    B. he is hanged
    C. he is drown

10. Who is made the captain in place of Jaggery?
    A. Barlow
    B. Charlotte
    C. Morgan

TURN HOMEWARD HANNALEE
Patricia Beatty

1. Where do Jem, Hannalee and Rosellen work?
   A. paper mill
   B. saw mill
   C. cloth mill

2. What does Hannalee's mother give her to help her remember to come home?
   A. persimmon seed button
   B. a locket
   C. a piece of lace

3. What does Hannalee give to Jem to wear on the trip north?
   A. her braids
   B. her coat
   C. her scarf

4. Where is Jeb sent to work in the North?
   A. in a factory
   B. on a farm
   C. in a country store

5. Who chooses not to return to the South?
   A. Hannalee
   B. Jem
   C. Rosellen

6. Where do Jem and Hannalee hide to watch the battle of Franklin?
   A. in a ditch
   B. up a sycamore tree
   C. in a barn loft

7. What work is Hannalee given in the North?
   A. factory worker
   B. seamstress
   C. household servant

8. Who is treated best by their new employers?
   A. Jem
   B. Rosellen
   C. Hannalee

9. Who helps Hannalee and Jem on the way home?
   A. a peddler with his wagon
   B. General William Sherman
   C. William Quantrill's Raiders

10. What happened to Davey in the war?
    A. he lost his arm
    B. he was killed
    C. he became a hero

THE TWISTED WINDOW
Lois Duncan

1. What does Brad want Tracy to do for him?
   A. find his baby sister
   B. rob a bank
   C. hide him

2. Who does Tracy live with?
   A. her grandparents
   B. her aunt and uncle
   C. her parents

3. How does Tracy meet Mindy?
   A. by babysitting for her
   B. at church
   C. in the park

4. What does Brad do to immobilize Doug Carver?
   A. tie him up
   B. lock him in the pantry
   C. knock him out

5. What happened to Tracy's mother?
   A. she ran away
   B. she was jailed
   C. she was knifed to death

6. While Brad is in Texas with Tracy where does he tell his mother he is?
   A. on vacation with Jamie
   B. visiting Washington D.C.
   C. fishing in Pecos

7. What identifying mark is Mindy supposed to have?
   A. a burn across her belly
   B. a birthmark on her back
   C. she's missing her right thumb

8. What happened to the real Mindy?
   A. she was kidnapped
   B. she was left on the roadside
   C. she was run over and killed by a car

9. Where does Brad hide out with Cricket?
   A. at the lake
   B. in his father's cabin
   C. on his aunt's farm

10. What causes Brad to realize he killed Mindy?
    A. a newspaper article
    B. seeing Cricket on the floor
    C. being hypnotized

UNDER ALIEN STARS
Pamela F. Service

1. What happened to Rogav Jy?
   A. he is given a party
   B. he is elected president
   C. he is kidnapped

2. What do Jason and Aryl climb in order to rescue their parents?
   A. the trash chute
   B. a mine shaft
   C. a sky scraper

3. What do Jason and Aryl cross a lake in?
   A. canoe
   B. sailboat
   C. speedboat

4. What happened to San Francisco?
   A. flooded
   B. fire bombed
   C. captured

5. What does Aryl wear to disguise herself?
   A. an overcoat
   B. a mask
   C. a checkered tablecloth

6. Who were the Hykzoi?
   A. friends of the Tsorians
   B. enemies of the Tsorians
   C. nobody

7. How does Aryl find the earth people?
   A. sophisticated
   B. boring
   C. primitive

8. How are Tsorian children raised?
   A. on ranches
   B. in nurseries
   C. with their parents

9. Where does Jason go when he needs to think?
   A. a cave in some rocks
   B. the lake
   C. his room

10. What is Jason's father?
    A. dead
    B. an officer in the military
    C. missing

UPCHUCK SUMMER'S REVENGE
Joel L. Schwartz

1. What happened to Richie on the way to camp?
   A. Oliver peed on him
   B. he threw up
   C. he had a flat tire

2. What does Jerry give Richie to wear while he cuts down the vines?
   A. raincoat
   B. zombie mask
   C. gorilla costume

3. Where does Uncle Marshall catch Richie and Chuck in the middle of the night?
   A. the girl's shower
   B. cafeteria stealing food
   C. highway hitch hiking home

4. Who does Richie write to on flowery stationary?
   A. his mother
   B. Jerry
   C. Lisa

5. What is in the letter Chuck writes to Jerry?
   A. an invitation
   B. a threat
   C. there is no tooth fairy

6. What does the loser of the football game have to do?
   A. eat a goldfish
   B. buy the winner pizza
   C. be the winner's personal slave

7. What does Lisa help Richie do?
   A. write football plays
   B. get a girl
   C. get revenge on Chuck

8. What does Jerry confess to Lisa?
   A. that he loves her
   B. he rigged the football game
   C. he's never kissed a girl

9. What sport does Richie's team look like they're playing during the football game?
   A. basketball
   B. volleyball
   C. baseball

10. What does Uncle Marshall check the football rule book to see?
    A. what happens when the ball is stolen
    B. what happens when the ball explodes
    C. what happens when there are only six men per team

THE VANDEMARK MUMMY
Cynthia Voigt

1. What is Althea scared of?
   A. boys
   B. getting lost
   C. the dark

2. Where is the collection stored?
   A. library basement
   B. museum of fine arts
   C. equipment locker

3. Where is the ambulance taking the mummy?
   A. to the hospital
   B. to the museum
   C. to the police station

4. Where is the stolen mummy found?
   A. swimming pool
   B. in the park
   C. back alley

5. What was deliberately damaged on the mummy?
   A. chest
   B. head
   C. feet

6. Who is kidnapped?
   A. Phineas
   B. Althea
   C. Dr. Hall

7. What does Phineas break?
   A. mirror
   B. wreath
   C. window

8. Who is O'Meara?
   A. college president
   B. reporter
   C. police officer

9. What does the kidnapper want from the mummy?
   A. poem
   B. necklace
   C. ransom

10. Who is the thief?
    A. Ken Simard
    B. Mr. Vandemark
    C. O'Meara

THE VOYAGE OF THE FROG
Gary Paulsen

1. What does David's uncle call waves?
   A. lumps
   B. power
   C. bumps

2. What does Owen not believe in?
   A. motors
   B. locks
   C. weather forecasts

3. What does the wooden boom do?
   A. hit David in the head
   B. break in half
   C. get struck by lightning

4. When David sees the storm what does he do?
   A. hide
   B. take down the sails
   C. panic

5. What does David hurt when he falls into the cabin?
   A. his head
   B. his leg
   C. his arm

6. Why was the shark attacking the boat?
   A. to sink it
   B. to play with it
   C. it was attracted to the flashing light

7. What does David find in a plastic bag?
   A. Owen's log
   B. a radio transmitter
   C. money

8. What almost ran into the boat at night?
   A. a giant sea turtle
   B. a submarine
   C. an oil tanker

9. What played with David as he sailed?
   A. a group of dolphins
   B. four killer whales
   C. sea gulls

10. When David sighted land where was he?
    A. San Francisco Bay
    B. Baja
    C. Mexico

THE WEIRDO
Theodore Taylor

1. How does Chip get burned?
   A. fireworks explosion
   B. house fire
   C. plane crash

2. Where is Sam when Chip first meets her?
   A. sitting on his roof
   B. sleeping in a tree stump
   C. working at the Dairy Queen

3. What does Chip keep in his cages?
   A. wounded birds
   B. wild bears
   C. rabbits

4. What is Chip's dad?
   A. big game hunter
   B. bird artist
   C. retired circus performer

5. What does Chip want Sam to do?
   A. marry him
   B. stay neutral and not take sides
   C. be hypnotized

6. What is Baron von Buckner?
   A. Sam's Uncle
   B. a hunting dog
   C. a bear

7. What does Sam do that makes her dad proud of her?
   A. she kills Henry
   B. she sides with the hunters
   C. she stands up to him

8. Who killed Alvin Howell and Tom Telford?
   A. Sam's father
   B. Buddy Bailey
   C. Jack Slade

9. Why was Alvin Howell killed?
   A. because of a gambling debt
   B. over a woman
   C. because he was poaching

10. What does Chip take off at the hunters meeting that he's never done in public before?
    A. hat and glove
    B. shoes
    C. shirt

WHERE IT STOPS, NOBODY KNOWS
Amy Ehrlick

1. What does Nina not like?
   A. apple pie
   B. wrestling
   C. horror movies

2. What school team does Nina play on?
   A. basketball team
   B. soccer team
   C. tennis team

3. What did Joyce sew with the needle and thread?
   A. Nina's thumb
   B. a dress
   C. the rip in the sofa

4. What does everyone do in Logan, Utah?
   A. gamble
   B. ride bikes
   C. ride horses

5. What does Nina collect?
   A. dolls
   B. stamps
   C. pictures of sunsets

6. What is Daryl Carpenter?
   A. nerd
   B. rocker
   C. jock

7. What did Nina's friend, Nancy, wear to McDonalds?
   A. formal dress
   B. costume
   C. pajamas

8. What did Nina receive that made her mother upset?
   A. kiss
   B. letter
   C. loan

9. What did Artie give Nina?
   A. silver earrings
   B. ring
   C. stuffed animal

10. Where did Joyce steal Nina from?
    A. hospital
    B. park
    C. supermarket

WHO KNEW THERE'D BE GHOSTS?
Bill Brittain

1. How did Essie die?
    A. she was shot in a holdup
    B. she died of small pox
    C. she drown

2. How was Thomas killed?
    A. he was beheaded by a sword
    B. he fell off a horse
    C. he died of rheumatic fever

3. Where do Essie and Thomas live in Parnell house?
    A. cellar
    B. attic
    C. ceiling

4. Where are Tommy, Books and Harry hiding when they hear Boots and Fancy Shoes talking?
    A. in a closet
    B. under a tree
    C. under the porch

5. What does Avery Katkus buy at an auction?
    A. Essie's emerald ring
    B. Thomas' flintlock
    C. Horace Parnell's journals

6. Where do Tommy, Books and Harry find the treasure?
    A. under the statue
    B. behind the mantel
    C. under the floorboards

7. How do Tommy, Books and Harry keep Avery Katkus from leaving the Parnell house?
    A. they tie him up
    B. they lock him in the closet
    C. they break the stairs

8. How does Avery Katkus keep the fifth council member away from the meeting?
    A. he kidnaps him
    B. he sends a fake telegram
    C. he pushes him over a cliff

9. What is the treasure that was in the lock box?
    A. a letter signed by the Continental Congress
    B. Horace's military papers
    C. Continental dollars

10. What does the mayor do with the treasure?
    A. keep it for the Parnell museum
    B. sell it
    C. give it to Tommy, Books and Harry

WHO PUT THAT HAIR IN MY TOOTHBRUSH?
Jerry Spinelli

1. What does Greg lie to his sister about?
   A. being chosen first
   B. about Paul liking her
   C. having a date with Jennifer Wade

2. What happened to Jennifer?
   A. she moved
   B. she ran away
   C. she broke her leg

3. Who does Megin give French crueller donuts to?
   A. Emilie in the nursing home
   B. Greg
   C. the girls at her party

4. What does Megin love to play?
   A. tennis
   B. hockey
   C. basketball

5. What do Megin's parents make her do?
   A. apologize to Greg
   B. stop seeing Emilie
   C. clean her room

6. What does Megin ask Emilie to be?
   A. her sister
   B. her honorary grandmother
   C. her adopted mother

7. What does Greg do all summer?
   A. work
   B. swim
   C. lift weights

8. What does Greg finally realize in the end?
   A. he likes Jennifer
   B. he likes Sara
   C. he likes Zoe

9. Why does Megin run off?
   A. because Emilie died
   B. she had a fight with Greg
   C. she lost the hockey game

10. What was Greg doing when he fell through the ice?
    A. getting Megin's hockey stick
    B. skating
    C. rescuing a dog

WILDERNESS PERIL
Thomas J. Dygard

1. Where does the money the boys found come from?
   A. ransom from a hijacking
   B. a bank robbery
   C. the lottery

2. What do the boys want to spend the reward money on?
   A. a flashy car
   B. college
   C. an apartment

3. What did the boys throw at the hijacker?
   A. the canoe
   B. a pan
   C. a jacket

4. What do the boys try to signal the plane with?
   A. a mirror
   B. a pan
   C. a jacket

5. What does the hijacker use to threaten the boys with?
   A. gun
   B. club
   C. knife

6. What does the hijacker ask a couple canoeing?
   A. if they have any food
   B. for a ride
   C. the name of the lake

7. Where do the boys hide the money?
   A. in the sleeping bags
   B. in a cave
   C. in a tree

8. What are the boys looking for when they find the money?
   A. bears
   B. water
   C. blueberries

9. What do the boys shine their flashlight on in the middle of the night?
   A. the hijacker
   B. a bear
   C. a raccoon

10. What does the hijacker do with his canoe?
    A. sink it
    B. cover it with ground cloth
    C. bury it

WINDCATCHER
Avi

1. What does Tony's grandmother give him that belonged to his grandfather?
    A. a model of the Swallow
    B. a fishing rod and reel
    C. a watch

2. Who is there a statue of at Haycock Point?
    A. Captain Swallow
    B. Captain Little John
    C. Captain Hook

3. What does Tony's grandmother buy for him?
    A. a compass and watch
    B. a map of the islands
    C. a pair of binoculars

4. When Tony asks the divers for directions what do they do?
    A. show him how to get home
    B. tell him to keep away
    C. ignore him

5. Who made Tony's model?
    A. his grandfather
    B. an antique dealer
    C. Ezra Little John

6. What do the divers do to warn Tony away?
    A. send a threatening letter
    B. show him their gun
    C. capsize his sailboat

7. What was Tony diving for between Hoghead and Money Island?
    A. his sneaker
    B. his compass
    C. treasure

8. What does Tony eat while he is stranded on an island?
    A. berries and nuts
    B. fish
    C. raw clams

9. Why is Tony stranded on the island?
    A. the snark is stolen
    B. the snark drifts away
    C. the snark is sunk

10. What does the couple offer Tony at first to keep the secret of the Swallow?
    A. to let him live
    B. ten thousand dollars
    C. to make him a partner

THE WINTER ROOM
Gary Paulsen

1. Why does Eldon hate the Spring?
   A. there is more work to do
   B. he has to quit school to plant crops
   C. manure thawing out stinks

2. How does Wayne try to get on the back of Stacker?
   A. jumping off the hayloft
   B. climbing from the fence
   C. using a stool

3. What was Uncle David?
   A. a woodcutter
   B. a farmer
   C. a butcher

4. What does Eldon hate about the fall?
   A. going back to school
   B. the killing
   C. the trip to the lake

5. What was Crazy Alen known for?
   A. setting the barn on fire
   B. kissing all the girls
   C. practical jokes

6. Why did Alen open his cabin door when he was about to die?
   A. so help could get in
   B. so his body would freeze solid
   C. so his dog could leave

7. How did the foreman get Alen's body out of the cabin?
   A. on a stretcher
   B. in a wheelbarrow
   C. by cutting the door bigger

8. How does Wayne hurt Uncle David?
   A. by spreading gossip about him
   B. by calling him a liar
   C. by hitting him

9. What does Uncle David do after Wayne hurts him?
   A. cut a log using two axes
   B. leave the farm
   C. stop speaking to Wayne

10. What does Crazy Alen do before he dies?
    A. lie on the floor spread eagle
    B. have his family come home
    C. throw a feast for his friends

THE WISH GIVER
Bill Brittain

1. What did Mr. Blinn give each person to make their wish come true?
   A. card with a red spot
   B. small mirror
   C. bottle with sand

2. What always gets in the way of Polly making friends?
   A. her dog
   B. her mouth
   C. her sense of humor

3. What did Polly do to make Eunice hate her?
   A. rip her dress
   B. tell lies about her
   C. hit her

4. What causes Polly to croak like a frog?
   A. spitting
   B. saying mean things
   C. flirting

5. What does Polly wish for?
   A. lots of talent
   B. lots of money
   C. lots of attention

6. What does Henry Piper lie to Rowena about?
   A. his wealth
   B. his age
   C. his travels

7. What does Henry Piper do for a living?
   A. sell farm implements
   B. sell pots and pans
   C. he's a handyman

8. How many spouts of water shoot up into the air by the house?
   A. 1
   B. 3
   C. 5

9. How does Adam get money to buy his parents a new farm?
   A. he goes to work for Stew Meat
   B. be becomes a dowser
   C. by trapping foxes

10. Who does Rowena start making a quilt for after the wishes are cancelled?
    A. Adam
    B. Sam
    C. Henry

WITH THE WIND, KEVIN DOLAN
Bryce Milligan

1. Why does Mr. Donohue pay for Tom and Kevin's passage to Texas?
    A. Kevin will marry his daughter, Rose
    B. he is their godfather
    C. Tom will work for him for one year

2. What does Tom do to stall the soldiers on their way to the Donohue's place?
    A. he cuts the cinches on their saddles
    B. he lets the soldiers' horses go
    C. he blocks the road

3. What happened to Owen's parents?
    A. they are run over by the soldier's horses
    B. they are put off their land
    C. they are hung as traitors

4. What gift does Owen give to Kevin?
    A. a hunting knife
    B. a flintlock rifle
    C. a book of Irish stories

5. Who dies of cholera?
    A. Brian
    B. Tom
    C. Mr. and Mrs. O'Mallory

6. Who helps Tom pick cactus thorns out of Kevin?
    A. Rose
    B. Karankawa Tom
    C. Mrs. Donohue

7. Who decides to become a cabin boy and live at sea?
    A. Brian
    B. Tom
    C. Owen

8. What did the letters Tom and Kevin receive say?
    A. Kevin and Tom's mother had a baby
    B. Mary was on her way to America
    C. their parents were killed by soldiers

9. What did Brian, Kevin and Owen learn from the first mate?
    A. how to navigate by the stars
    B. how to carve a flute
    C. how to spit

10. What do Brian, Kevin and Tom give the Donohue's for Christmas?
    A. cloth and tobacco
    B. needles and a hunting knife
    C. flower seeds and a new pipe

THE WOLVES OF WILLOUGHBY CHASE
Joan Aiken

1. What caused the window on the train to break?
   A. train wreck
   B. Mr. Grimshaw's fist
   C. wolves

2. What does Sylvia's aunt not want her brother to know?
   A. she is poor
   B. she has a criminal record
   C. she is married

3. What is wrong with Mr. Grimshaw?
   A. he lost his memory
   B. he was bitten by a wolf
   C. he lost a leg in the war

4. What disaster were Bonnie's parents in?
   A. a hurricane
   B. a shipwreck
   C. a mud slide

5. What does Miss Slighcarp try to do?
   A. teach the girls to be ladies
   B. be a substitute mother to the girls
   C. steal Sir Willoughby's home and fortune

6. What happened to Bonnie and Sylvia their first day at the orphanage?
   A. they were locked in a closet
   B. their hair was cut off
   C. they were beaten

7. What do Sylvia and Bonnie sleep in on the way to London?
   A. a meadow with sheep
   B. a hay loft
   C. a cart with geese

8. Where do the police hide to spy on Miss Slighcarp?
   A. under the window
   B. in a secret passage in the wall
   C. in the bedroom closet

9. What do Miss Slighcarp and Mrs. Brisket turn Willoughby Chase into?
   A. a boarding house and school
   B. a nightclub
   C. a hotel and restaurant

10. What does Mr. Grimshaw do in London at night?
    A. break into Aunt Jane's room
    B. plan to sink a ship
    C. kill Sir Willoughby's attorney

WONDER
Rachel Vail

1. What does Jessica do with her penny?
   A. throw it in a wishing well
   B. rub it for good luck
   C. tape it to her belly button

2. What do Jessica, Connor, and Jordan do at the crik?
   A. have a mud fight
   B. fish
   C. tell ghost stories

3. What died causing Jessica to cry?
   A. bird
   B. fish
   C. cat

4. Who does Jessica date?
   A. Jordan
   B. Connor
   C. Benjamin

5. Why is Jessica's father upset?
   A. his marriage is in trouble
   B. he wrecked his car
   C. the business is bad

6. What costume does Jessica use for Halloween?
   A. a California raisin
   B. a loaf of wonder bread
   C. a giant orange

7. What do Tracy and Jessica buy at the mall?
   A. shoes
   B. lipstick
   C. bras

8. What do the students say over and over when they have a sub?
   A. hack
   B. chop
   C. quit

9. Where is Jessica when she gets her first kiss?
   A. at a party
   B. in school
   C. on her front porch

10. What does Jessica do with the dress her mother bought her?
    A. throw it away
    B. give it to Goodwill
    C. cut it up

THE YEAR WITHOUT MICHAEL
Beth Pfeffer

1. What do Jerry Murphy and Jody say whenever they want to cry?
    A. David Templeton
    B. Twinkle, Twinkle, Little Star
    C. Have a good one

2. Where is Michael's father when Michael disappears?
    A. at the store
    B. at the cabin
    C. at the office

3. What were Michael and Jody talking about just before his disappearance?
    A. their parent's marriage
    B. their report cards
    C. their upcoming vacation

4. How many people come to Kay's birthday party?
    A. ten
    B. none
    C. five

5. Who does Jody's grandmother blame for Michael's leaving?
    A. Michael's school
    B. Michael's father
    C. Michael's mother

6. Who are Jody's best friends?
    A. Kay and Jerry
    B. Jerry and Lauren
    C. Lauren and Maris

7. Who gets kicked out of the house?
    A. Kay
    B. Maris
    C. Jody

8. Who hires a private detective?
    A. the school
    B. the parents
    C. the grandmother

9. What does Jody do that helps her forget Michael for a little while?
    A. go to a dance
    B. be in the school play
    C. read a book

10. Where does Jody go to look for Michael?
    A. the farm
    B. New York City
    C. the subway

YOUR MOVE, J.P.!
Lois Lowry

1. Where is Angela from?
   A. South America
   B. a ranch in Wyoming
   C. London, England

2. What does Angela say her father is?
   A. a genetics doctor
   B. a salesman
   C. a plumber

3. What does J.P. pretend to have?
   A. triple framosis
   B. a blood disease
   C. a brain tumor

4. What do J.P. and Ralph name for each letter of the alphabet?
   A. song titles
   B. diseases
   C. places

5. What can J.P. not do in his costume?
   A. eat
   B. walk
   C. sit down

6. What is the theme of all the costumes supposed to be?
   A. winter
   B. spring
   C. fall

7. What causes Ray Burke Thaxter to die?
   A. the Vietnam War
   B. a rare disease
   C. a boating accident

8. What do Ray Burke Thaxter's parents build in Ray's honor?
   A. a hospital
   B. a science lab
   C. a statue

9. Why does Hope disguise herself in J.P.'s costume and play in the tournament in his place?
   A. because J.P. is in the park
   B. because J.P. had to go home
   C. because J.P. is locked in the restroom

10. Why does J.P. have a bootie on his head?
    A. so he won't be distracted
    B. to keep his ears warm
    C. to be a mugger

ANSWER KEYS

FORM A

1. C
2. A
3. A
4. B
5. C
6. B
7. C
8. B
9. A
10. A

FORM B

1. A
2. B
3. A
4. B
5. C
6. C
7. A
8. C
9. B
10. B

AUTHOR/TITLE INDEX

TITLES BY SUBJECT INDEX